HOW TO MAKE LIFE
EASY FOR YOURSELF

How to Make Life Easy For Yourself

DENISE KATZ

Foreword by Maureen Lipman

ANGUS
& ROBERTSON
PUBLISHERS

To my mother, with love

ACKNOWLEDGEMENTS

I would like to thank the following for their invaluable help:
Gloria Ferris, my agent, without whom the book wouldn't have come to fruition, Valerie Hudson, my marvellous editor (Editorial Director at Angus & Robertson), who polished my pearls with patience, panache and always good humour, Esther Jagger for her invaluable help on gardening and many other matters, Maureen Lipman who wrote the magnificent foreword to my book, and my wonderful sister Wendy, my most ardent supporter, who encouraged me from concept to conclusion.

ANGUS & ROBERTSON PUBLISHERS

16 Golden Square, London WIR 4BN,
United Kingdom and
Unit 4, Eden Park, 31 Waterloo Road,
North Ryde, NSW, Australia 2113.

First published in the United Kingdom by
Angus & Robertson (UK) in 1990
First published in Australia by
Angus & Robertson Publishers in 1990

Text copyright © Denise Katz 1990
Illustrations copyright © Frank Rodgers 1990

Typeset in Great Britain by AKM Associates (UK) Ltd
Printed in Finland

British Library Cataloguing in Publication Data

Katz, Denise
  How to Make Life Easy For Yourself.
  1. Personal success
  I. Title
  158'.1

  ISBN 0 207 16578 5

CONTENTS

FOREWORD

As I fumble through impenetrable drawers in search of the only pen in the house which hasn't dried up through being left lidless in an impenetrable drawer, it occurs to me that, had I read Denise Katz's book on 'organisation' just a few decades ago, I might have a well-stocked and neatly tabulated pen drawer and this introduction might have been written marginally before the seventh deadline date for its delivery had twice passed me and its publishers by.

I first encountered Denise's name in the *Evening Standard* in an article about her creative organisation of Fenella Fielding's wardrobe. Now I know Fenella. I have seen her getting made-up, and if the inside of her wardrobe was anything remotely akin to the inside of her make-up bag, I could only assume that Ms Katz had an exploratory daring which made Dame Freya Stark look insular. I know Fenella wouldn't mind my saying this because I am possibly the only person in London whose wardrobe invites one question only, and that is: 'Did the burglars get away with much else besides clothes?'

It's a fact known to even those mortals who have not yet sojourned in the Betty Ford Clinic that you cannot straighten up your mind if you cannot straighten up your own room. The Denise Katz way of organisation may start from the opposite premise, but it gets the same results. And it's cheaper. I called up Denise to galvanise rather than organise me into planning my son's Barmitzvah a mere eight months ahead. I was playing my one-woman show *Re:Joyce* each night at the theatre and my one-woman show *Re:Morse* each day at home. I'd made a few desultory enquiries but found myself paralysed between two styles – vintage and classic. Should I go Rosenthal's *Barmitzvah Boy* and start carving a model of my thirteen-year-old son out of chopped herring – or should I find a discreet candle-lit room somewhere and hire a harpist? Enter Ms Katz. Briefcase in hand, Filofax at fingertips, neat navy suit and sensible, intelligent even, shoes.

Over a period of two months Denise did the dialling. She also did the trudging and the inquisition and the shopping for bargains and the phoning in of results. In fact she did the real-life equivalent of what I do on the BT ads. with equal enthusiasm, but, one hopes, a little more restraint. Without too much pain, by the time I was due to depart for a trip to Australia I had four totally differing venues booked for four totally different types of Bar-mitzvah. All I had to do was choose. This proved so hard that Denise did the only thing possible. She found me a fifth. Over-emotionally and with enormous relief, I took it.

Then she packed my cases for Australia. Greater love for the job hath no creative organiser than to pack four cases for four Rosenthals of various ages, egos and degrees of tastelessness. Piles of summer clothing had lain on our bedroom floor for weeks, and I'd taken to jumping over them Kanga-style rather than doing anything in the way of selection – let alone packing them. Ms Katz moved into action. She stripped the wardrobe of plastic clothes wrapping, stuffed every shoe with every knicker and bra, and introduced me and my rumpled family to the joys of crush-free packing. A joy from which I've never looked back. Layers of coordinated clothes, each one covered in polythene wrapping, came out 'down-under' looking exactly as they'd gone in 'up-over'. Revelation. And I don't mean the suitcase. The fact that the summer weather in Australia was the worst for twenty years, with rain, gales and – wait for it – snow in Perth, and that I spent the two weeks wearing three T-shirts at a time and one wet rumpled blazer which had to be wrung out in Melbourne and disposed of in Bangkok, is no reflection at all on the choice of the garments she and I eventually selected.

Some time later, whilst still on Barmitzvah business, Denise popped round with a list of musicians and cake suppliers, and ended up packing the Rosenthals once again for a fortnight in the Italian Lakes – the ensuing article about which, three months later, I've yet to deliver. I've just about caught on to her method of packing, but the ability to pack in a fully organised day eludes me still. Maybe I should read this excellent book again. Better still, maybe I should learn it. If that doesn't help, I'll eat my words. Maybe I'll eat *her* words. Page by page. In a highly 'organised' fashion.

Maureen Lipman

INTRODUCTION

In 1988, after various jobs in retailing and office management, I set up the Creative Organizing Service, advising all sorts of people – some famous, some not so famous – on how to plan their time and their money in such a way that they'll be relaxed, stress-free – and organised!

Since then so many clients have asked me to put it all down on paper that I decided to write *How to Make Life Easy For Yourself*.

If you answer yes to three or more of the following questions, you, too, need this book:

	No	Yes
Are you ever late for appointments?		
Have you ever lost the keys to: • your home • your car • your office?		
Have you ever left your umbrella in: • a train • a bus • a restaurant?		
Do you often pay library fines?		
Have you ever forgotten a friend's birthday?		
Have you ever failed to return an important phone call?		

	No	Yes
Do you panic when faced with an unexpected guest for dinner?		
Do you ever run out of money?		
Do you ever arrive late at work?		

Here's another way of looking at the problem:

	No	Yes
How many of the following do you have/use?		

- diary ⎫ or Filofax
- address book ⎭
- monthly budgeting plan
- duplicate make-up bag with duplicate make-up
- list of things to do/buy
- plastic or manilla folders
- highlighter pens
- Post-Its

Do you always carry a pen with you (or are you one of those annoying people who hold everyone up in the supermarket)?

Do you keep spares of the following items handy?
- toilet rolls
- kitchen rolls
- soap
- toothpaste
- tampons
- tights
- stamps

If you end up with less than 5 yeses, you need this book, so read on . . .

1 Planning Makes Perfect – Why You Need This Book

FIVE GOLDEN RULES

I wasn't born organised. I just decided to become so, after too much fury with myself for always losing my bus pass and door keys, and continually getting to work late. So one day I took myself to task. I learnt that it's easy to be organised. If you can clean your teeth you can do it – and you've probably been cleaning your teeth by yourself, without giving it a second thought, since you were five.

So don't despair if up till now you've lived your life in total chaos. Just apply my five golden rules:

- DO IT NOW
- BE PREPARED
- WORK AT YOUR OWN PACE
- DON'T AIM FOR PERFECTION
- SORT OUT YOUR PRIORITIES

and take control of your life. By the end of this book you will see just how easy it is to apply the principles of organisation, which will:

- leave you twice as much free time, and
- allow others to see you as a reliable person

Be prepared

This is the key to organisation. It is:

- never forgetting a birthday
- never missing a deadline

- never running out of milk . . . or anything else
- always arriving on time
- always arriving at your destination with everything you need

Do it now

The biggest enemy of organisation is procrastination. We all know how easy it is to phone a friend instead of paying our bills, but remember, if you don't do it now:

- it may take twice the time
- it may cost you more
- you may lose your credibility
  and worst of all
- you'll be adding yet another piece of clutter to your mind

Work at your own pace

If the thought of dusting all the books on your sixteen bookshelves puts you off even starting the job, try and do two shelves a day – in other words work at your own pace. Just don't procrastinate – make a start now.

Don't aim for perfection

The reason why so many people put things off is because they aim for perfection. But you're not in a competition, and surely the only prize is a sense of satisfaction at having completed a task. If you set sensible goals for yourself, rather than impossible ones, you're much more likely to discover the satisfaction of having achieved them.

Sort out your priorities

This is the area where people find the most difficulty.

Indeed, faced with three things to do, many people get so confused that they end up doing none of them. Always think about the most efficient way of doing a job – e.g. if, in the course of an evening, you have three things to take upstairs, take them all together instead of making three separate trips. But do make sure you don't turn this common sense approach to doing tasks into an excuse for putting them off!

EVERYONE CAN BENEFIT

This book is aimed primarily at women, who still seem to be the chief pickers up and putters away, the budget-makers and the planners – certainly in the domestic sphere. But that doesn't mean to say that there aren't very many tidy efficient men – or, even more important, *would-be* tidy and efficient men. House-husbands and men living on their own can become better organised and lead an easier, more streamlined life by following the advice in this book. And even those who do have a wife or girlfriend or mother around them might well benefit from learning not to rely on others to do everything for them!

DOING IT YOUR WAY

Finally, the advice and techniques offered in this book are the ones that work best for me, and have worked well on lots of my clients. But everyone has a different lifestyle, with different daily priorities, so don't be afraid to adapt some of these ideas. Follow them to the letter if that makes you feel happiest, but equally feel free to use them as a starting point if you prefer. After all, the intention is to make *your* life easier for *you*.

2 About the House

Whether you spend all day at home looking after small children, or whether you're out of it for twelve hours a day doing a job, your home should be a peaceful haven that functions properly. It's hard to put your feet up and relax after a hard day if the armchairs are full of last week's newspapers, or to get the kids' lunch if you didn't shop properly and there's nothing in the house that they'll eat. So let's start off with a big, helpful hint-filled chapter on organising one of the most important places in everyone's life.

MAKE THE BEST OF YOUR HOME

- by filling it with flowers, bulbs or plants
- by ensuring your net curtains always look freshly laundered

....
TIP

Keep flowers fresh and longer-lasting by changing the water regularly and at the same time cutting a bit off the stems. Nothing makes a room look worse than a vase full of brown, drooping flowers
....
TIP

Make sure there are enough power points around the house – extensions and adaptors aren't very satisfactory and can easily get overloaded and therefore dangerous. If your home falls short in this respect, get an electrician in to add some extra sockets
....

KITCHEN TALK

In most homes the kitchen is the power house. It's where possibly the largest number of activities take place – food preparation, cooking, washing, ironing, washing up and often eating too – yet it's often, after the loo, the smallest room in the house. It's also the room where the greatest number of accidents in the home occur. Clearly it's a prime candidate for an organising hand to help turn this potential trouble spot into a streamlined and efficient place that's a pleasure to work in.

The secret of having an optimally organised kitchen is to keep only the utensils you really need. That doesn't mean you should throw away a chip pan or fish fryer which you don't use on a regular basis. But there's absolutely no reason to keep old lids which don't fit any of your existing saucepans – 'just in case they come in useful'.

....

TIP
When you move home, don't pack up all your crockery, glassware and china only to discard a lot of it at the other end. It's amazing how much accumulates over the years that is never used but just gets transported from one home to the next. Weed it out before you move, and either sell it or give it to a charity shop
....

The more organised your kitchen, the more you'll be able to store in it. Here's a quiz to find out the state of *your* kitchen!

Q. Do all your saucepans have matching fitting lids?
A. *For yes, score 5. For no, score 0.*

Q. Where in the kitchen do you keep your kitchen roll?
A. *Near the sink, score 5. Anywhere else, score 0.*

Q. Does your fridge door open on the most convenient side?

A. *For yes, score 5. For no, score 0.*

Q. Where is your oven cloth kept in relation to the oven?

A. *Very near, score 5. Fairly near, score 5. Anywhere else, score 0.*

Q. How many of the following items do you keep in regular stock and have in your kitchen now?
- aluminium foil
- kitchen roll
- clean tea towels
- airtight containers for tea, coffee, sugar
- bottled water
- floor cloth
- broom
- dustpan and brush
- soap
- hand cream
- watering can for pot plants

A. *For every yes, score 3. For every no, score 0.*

Q. Have you got any dirty dishes in the sink?

A. *For no, score 5. For just a mug, or a cup and saucer, score 2. For more than that, score 0.*

Scores: 50 plus. You have a well-organised and hygienic kitchen. Congratulations!

40–50. You are well on the way to running a well-equipped kitchen, but do try to keep to the basic requirements.

Less than 40. There's room for improvement . . .

To derive maximum efficiency from your kitchen, it must be well organised, equipped with practical items which are easily cleaned and – above all – planned with a view to safety.

Mistakes people make

- they arrange the contents of their kitchen without any thought – for instance, they keep the oven cloth on a hook near the sink and not by the cooker where it's needed
- they make life harder than they need by not washing up as they go – so the fat congeals and the food dries hard on the plates. It's not easy to enjoy watching TV when you know you've got to tackle a sink full of dirty dishes – later . . .
- they have no back-up system to replace items as they are used
- the kitchen isn't planned with sufficient thought about how far people have to walk to perform simple routine tasks

Kitchen Planning

Make sure your kitchen suits your family's requirements.

- ask yourself how often you will be using it all together
- which items of standard kitchen equipment do you use: cooker, microwave, fridge, freezer, dishwasher, washing machine, tumble drier? Do you need any extra ones?
- are your existing items of equipment in the most sensible places (e.g. don't let your microwave take up valuable work surface – try and put it in a place where you wouldn't normally want to prepare food. And is your fridge perhaps too near your cooker for efficiency?)

If you aren't pleased with your kitchen, take a good look at it – you might be surprised at how few changes are needed to make it function more effectively, e.g.:

- hanging the fridge or washing machine door on the other side
- adding more electrical sockets
- putting in an extractor fan
- moving the breakfast table under the lights

To make the most of a small kitchen, build upwards – have lots of wall units. If you really would feel happier having your kitchen extended or radically changed, call in a professional. Their experience is worth paying for – often they can see better solutions to your problems than you can.

Make things easy for yourself

....
TIP
Keep a tin or box of spare electric fuses – 2 amp, 5 amp and 13 amp
....

- if you wash or sweep your kitchen floor daily there's no time for dirt to build up – and it's more hygienic too. Do things before they become twice as difficult
- keep the kitchen roll near the sink
- fill saucepans with water as soon as you've removed the food from them. This makes them much easier to wash up – no caked-on food
- store regularly used items near the front of your cupboards. There's no point in keeping the cereal boxes behind the tomato sauce, but you'd be surprised how many people do!
- keep the kettle and mugs near the coffee, tea and sugar jars
- keep saucepans in floor cupboards, and items which aren't used so often (such as soup bowls) in higher cupboards

- from the point of view of storage, dishes which stack are best
- keep cutlery neatly separated in divided cutlery trays
- make sure your kitchen table or other work surface is at a comfortable height
- try to equip your kitchen with as many tiled surfaces as you can, because they're easy to wipe down and keep clean. Particularly have them around the cooker, so greasy spatter marks can be dealt with quickly

Safety in the kitchen

- make sure you've got really good lighting in the right place, and enough of it
- don't leave saucepan handles sticking out from the cooker top where they can be pulled over by children's hands or by getting caught in sleeves or aprons
- if you have children, get a telescopic flex for your kettle or (better still buy a cordless kettle – they aren't expensive
- again if you have children, choose household cleaning products with child-resistant closures. Some poisonous products are given a bitter taste so children who try them spit them out
- keep kitchen knives out of children's reach
- keep all cleaning materials, chemicals etc. in cupboards above child height
- read instructions on cleaning materials carefully – lots of them shouldn't be mixed with other substances such as detergents, for instance, or a nasty gas may be produced
- don't use slippery polish on the kitchen floor
- have a first aid kit handy in the kitchen. It should contain at least plasters and an antiseptic like Savlon

or TCP to deal with cuts and burns

Kitchen pegboard

This is the single most useful and efficient piece of equipment to make any home run smoothly. On it will be attached your

- shopping requirement chart (see pp. 32–34)
- message chart
- diary chart

SHOPPING REQUIREMENT CHART
This is where you fill in regular items as they run out as well as special items you will need for the coming week.

Use the chart I have devised for you as a basis. Take from it the items you use regularly, and make some photocopies. Fill out one every week and take it with you on every trip to the supermarket.

MESSAGE CHART
This doesn't need to be any more than a large sheet of paper. On it you write any messages you want to leave for other members of the family and any messages taken down from the phone. Make sure you include the date and time. Each person just has to check the board whenever he or she comes into the house.

DIARY CHART
Like the other two charts, this must be kept up-to-date, so that before making social or business arrangements you can check on everyone else's plans or whereabouts. Large stationers sell suitable charts for this purpose. Buy one well before Christmas every year, so you won't find stocks have run out, and then immediately fill in any known engagements for the coming year, e.g. dental appointments, holiday dates, and when to have the car MOTd.

SHORT OF SPACE?
If you haven't got room for a pegboard in the kitchen, buy the largest, clearest calendar you can accommodate instead of a diary chart. Your shopping chart and messages can be attached to the fridge door with magnets.

Fridge/freezer

Along with your microwave and washing machine, your fridge/freezer, used properly, has got to be one of the most valuable pieces of equipment in any kitchen.
- make sure your fridge is cold enough (it should

always be below 5°C/41°F, while freezers should be at 0°C/32°F. And remember each time you open the fridge door the inside temperature rises – so don't leave the door open for longer than necessary

- make sure you defrost regularly (if it doesn't do so automatically), so that it works at maximum efficiency
- defrost and clean when stocks of food are at their lowest, keeping the remaining food as cold as possible.
- label and date food in the freezer – keeping the door open while you are rummaging around anonymous packages makes ice build up, and as a result you have to defrost more often
- keep a freezer book in which you enter everything you freeze (type of food, date frozen, number of portions if not obvious). That way you'll know what's in the freezer even before you open the door, and there won't be any ancient relics kicking around in it. Tick items off as you use them
- be organised about the way you use food – make sure you use older stocks of the same items first
- keep raw and cooked food separately in the fridge. Make sure raw meat and food that's defrosting are put at the bottom of the fridge so they can't drip on to other food

Storing food the organised way

- don't store food near heat (e.g. radiators or the cooker) or in full sunlight – the vitamin content will be damaged
- buy soft fruit and green vegetables little and often and keep in the fridge
- potatoes and harder vegetables keep longer – put them in a cool, dark, dry place

- eat fresh fish quickly – though it will keep for 1 day in a plastic bag in the fridge
- raw meat will keep in the fridge for 2–3 days
- cooked meat should not be kept in the fridge for more than 1 day
- dairy products keep for at least 1 week in the fridge – keep butter and cheese in their wrappers or in covered containers so they don't exchange smells with other foods
- vegetable oils need to be kept cool – don't keep them near the cooker
- keep dry goods such as flour and salt in dry, sealed containers in a cool cupboard. Flour will keep in this way for at least 2 months
- keep herbs and spices in airtight containers too – whole ones keep much better than ground

....

TIP
To reseal cereal packets use a clothes peg

....

Kitchen hygiene musts

- don't allow pets near food or on worktops
- wash pets' dishes and utensils separately from your own
- wash your hands in warm water and soap before handling food, after touching pets, dirty nappies and the pedal bin, and after going to the loo
- put plasters on all cuts and grazes on your hands
- wash out your tea towels and dishcloths frequently
- wash worktops, chopping boards and utensils frequently in hot soapy water and dry them thoroughly, preferably with disposable paper towels
- don't use the same knife or chopping board for raw meat, cooked food and fresh vegetables without washing them in between. Ideally, keep one board specifically for raw meat and have a separate one for other foods

Avoid those tummy bugs!

- thaw frozen food thoroughly – in the fridge or microwave is safest, as a warm kitchen encourages bacteria growth. Poultry in particular (and especially large items such as the Christmas turkey) should always be defrosted completely before cooking
- always follow package instructions, especially when microwaving (follow manufacturer's instructions here, too)
- remember to cook meat thoroughly
- cooked food should not be left to cool for more than 1 hour before putting it into the fridge or freezer
- food should never be reheated more than once, and even then it must be piping hot and cooked right through

....
TIP
Make sure the environmental health officer (look in the phone book, under the name of your local authority) knows of any foul drains
....
TIP
Take used bottles to a bottle bank
Recycle anything else you can – your local public rubbish tip should have facilities for dealing with scrap metal, newspapers, wood etc.
....

SHOPPING AHEAD

Do you ever:
- run out of milk
- find your bread has gone stale and your cheese has grown mould?
- have no food to offer an unexpected guest?

None of these things need ever happen if you follow two of my golden rules: DO IT NOW and BE PREPARED.
- use a model list of the things you should always try to have in the house and keep it in a prominent place in the kitchen
- plan your food requirements for the coming week
- keep a running list of items you're just about to run out of on a pad of paper specially for the purpose
- buy larger sizes of non-perishables such as detergent – it's more economical and it cuts down on the number of shopping trips. But first make sure your kitchen cupboards will accommodate them!

Follow these tips and you'll save yourself a lot of time, money and energy. Shopping is basically pretty boring and pretty tiring, but there's nothing more irritating than finding you've lugged all those carrier bags home only to find you've forgotten that essential item that made you go to the supermarket in the first place!

Once you've armed yourself with all the right lists and made sure you've got enough time and money for a proper shop, there's still a lot that can go wrong. But by thinking ahead and planning your time you'll soon find that regular and organised shopping trips will become second nature to you.

Be a proper shopper

- buy a large container of milk, divide into portions and freeze. Each night take out a portion to defrost for use next day. You can do this with orange juice, too
- buy large quantities of essentials like hard cheese and bread, and freeze it in small quantities so you only have to take out what you need each day
- have a few pre-prepared frozen meals – for 1, 2, and 4 people – on standby in the freezer, so you've always got something to offer unexpected guests
- try to do your big supermarket shops early in the day – you'll get fresher food, you'll feel fresher, and there's a better chance the shops won't be so crowded
- keep your supermarket plastic carrier bags – and remember to take them with you next time you shop!
- keep a supply of longer-lasting adaptable foods like rice, crackers or crispbread and some basic tinned foods
- take a calculator to the shops – it will enable you to compare weight-for-price on different sizes and brands

Be a safe shopper

- always check sell-by dates on food, avoid damaged packs, and don't buy dirty or cracked eggs
- don't buy from shops which don't look clean (that includes their staff – there should be no smoking in the food section)

- don't forget to put in the fridge as soon as possible things that need to be kept cool – don't leave them for hours in the car
- make sure meat is wrapped and kept separately from the other foods in your shopping bag

The essential shopping chart

ESSENTIAL ESSENTIALS
Milk
Bread
Coffee
Tea
Sugar
Butter/margarine

DAIRY PRODUCTS
Cream
Yoghurt
Cheese/cheese spread
Eggs

DRINKS
Bottled water
Fruit juices
Squash
Wine
Beer
Mixers

MEAT
Beef (joint/steak/casserole/mince)
Lamb (joint/chops/casserole)
Chicken (whole/pieces)
Pork (joint/chops)
Liver
Kidneys
Sausages

FISH
Fresh

Tinned
Smoked

VEGETABLES
Potatoes
Onions
Greens
Root vegetables
Tomatoes
Salad stuff

FRUIT
Apples
Pears
Grapefruit
Oranges
Bananas
Grapes
Melon

FROZEN AND TINNED GOODS
Peas
Green beans
Sweetcorn
Tomato juice
Fruit salad
Baked beans
Tomatoes
Soup
Pastry

DRY GOODS
Rice
Pasta
Pulses
Dried fruits

Flour (plain/self-raising)
Cereals
Crispbread
Spices
Salt/pepper
Biscuits

HOUSEHOLD GOODS
Toilet paper
Washing powder/liquid
Washing-up liquid
Fabric softener
Kitchen towels
Aluminium foil
Clingfilm
Dishcloths
Disinfectant
Air freshener
Lavatory cleaner
Toothpaste
Soap
Tampons
Deodorant
Light bulbs
Bin liners

SPECIAL INTEREST
Pet food
Cat litter
Baby food
Nappies

Use this as a basic chart and add to or delete items from it until it becomes tailor-made for your own requirements. For instance, if different members of your family eat different breakfast cereals, you'll want to name them individually rather than just have a blanket heading 'cereals'. There's also a more detailed list of bathroom and toilet requisites on p.42 which you might want to amalgamate with this one. When you've worked out your list, have some photocopies made at a local copy shop and take a filled-out copy of the list with you every time you do a supermarket shop.

....

TIP
For a quick, in-between-times shopping trip, make a short list on the perforated card from tissue boxes or the sheets of card you often get in tights packets (they won't get crumpled or accidentally thrown away like scraps of paper might)
....

Shopping for the elderly

Elderly or disabled people often don't get enough to eat, perhaps because they live alone and have no one to do their shopping, or because there is no supermarket nearby. If you know someone who has this problem you can help them by making sure they always have bread substitutes available, such as crispbread or cream crackers. Rice and cereals are good energy-providers that keep well. To go with them buy powdered or long-life milk. Fruit juice should be bought in bottles, cans or foil-lined cartons suitable for indefinite storage. Bottled water also keeps for a long time.

Tinned foods (e.g. stews, vegetables, rice pudding) are especially useful. They side-step the possibility of not thawing frozen food properly, they keep well outside a fridge, they usually need little extra cooking, and if you buy only small sizes old people won't have half a tin left over which they might be tempted to store for too long.

TIPS FOR TIDINESS

To keep your house respectable with minimum effort:

- do housework weekly, and WORK AT YOUR OWN PACE
- carry all small cleaning equipment round the house with you in an apron with several large pockets
- make sure larger equipment is readily accessible and easily assembled – even ironing won't seem such a chore if the ironing board is easy to get at
- no time for a complete clean-up? Polish one thing beautifully, e.g. a silver jug, and fill it with flowers. DON'T AIM FOR PERFECTION
- dust from top to bottom – otherwise dust will fall on the areas you've already done
- try to get the vacuum cleaner round at least once a week, especially in areas of heavy traffic
- don't run out of vacuum cleaner bags
- get as much as you can off the floor and under cover – e.g. put shoes in a cupboard or shoe rack where they won't pick up dust
- keep ornaments to a minimum – have just the things you like best, keep them clean and therefore enjoy them
- always screw back tops on jars and bottles, e.g. nail varnish, orange squash and Tippex, immediately after use to save disaster later. DO IT NOW
- throw out newspapers daily (in a pile for recycling)
- deal with clothes immediately you take them off:
  - if clean, put back in the wardrobe or drawer
  - if dirty and washable, put in the laundry basket
  - if dirty and not washable, put in the hall ready to take to the cleaners next day
  - repair anything which needs attention. Don't put it back in the wardrobe only to bring it out again in the same state

- throw away letters after answering them. Keep (and file) only those that are really important, e.g. tax, insurance etc.
- put away shopping immediately you get home

Organise your videos and cassettes

Label clearly what you have recorded with:
- date
- title
- artist
- length of recording
- amount of recording time left

Then file them away:
- all facing the same way
- all with their titles clearly visible

Organise your books

There are lots of ways of organising books. If yours are just for pleasure (i.e. lots of novels) and you never need to consult one in a hurry, they can look pretty arranged according to colour. Otherwise, the most effective method is usually this:
- divide them into subject areas
- divide them alphabetically by author within these subject areas
- do the same, as far as possible, with over-size books that won't fit on your bookshelves but have to go on a table or in a cupboard elsewhere
- keep frequently consulted books (e.g. dictionary, home medical encyclopaedia) very handy
- cookery books are often best kept in the kitchen – but well away from likely cooking splashes

Clean them once a year:
- remove books a few at a time
- dust shelves
- clean books with the nozzle attachment of a vacuum cleaner (stops you pushing dust between the pages or down the spine)

....
TIP

When clearing up the living area, get as much as you can off the floor – it's psychologically depressing to see the floor cluttered. Put up shelves or, if you're short of space, hooks on which you can hang things in clear plastic bags tied with coloured rope – this is particularly good for children's things
....
TIP

To stop your bedroom looking untidy, always hang your dressing gown either in your wardrobe or in the bathroom
....

MY BED HAS GOT TO BE HERE SOMEWHERE!

HIGH-SPEED DEEP CLEANING

Once a year most of us like to try and get the place looking really nice and fresh. The concept of spring cleaning may seem a bit old-fashioned, but undoubtedly those rays of spring sunshine do show up shabby paintwork and the places you couldn't quite reach with the vacuum cleaner. Here's a step-by-step plan to help you deal with this chore. Some of the items you may also want to incorporate into your more frequent cleaning routines, depending on how much time you have available.

- shake rugs and mats
- brush ceilings
- brush walls and picture rails
- clean window sills, skirting boards and other gloss-painted areas such as doors with warm water and a proprietary cleaner, then rinse and dry
- dust or wash ornaments (discarding any you're tired of)
- dust and polish furniture and mirrors
- clean inside drawers and reline them (discarding items you don't like or don't wear)
- remove and wash net curtains
- clean windows. Fill a bucket with warm water and washing-up liquid, wring out a chamois-type cloth in it and work from the outer edge inwards. With a second dampish cloth run the windows from side to side and rinse with cold water, then leave to dry. Change the water frequently. Only tackle the outsides of the windows yourself if you are fairly athletic and your windows aren't too far above the ground. Otherwise play safe and get a window cleaner to do it
- vacuum mattresses, upholstered furniture, cushions and curtains
- wash curtains if they are washable, also cushion

covers; if not washable, send them to the cleaners
- vacuum carpets, then shampoo them
- soft furnishings and carpets benefit from occasional steam cleaning by a specialist firm (once a year if you can afford it)
- if your rooms are beginning to look tired (or you are tired of them) give them a single coat of emulsion paint, if appropriate, or consider redecorating in a new colour scheme altogether

....

TIP

Don't put rugs on polished floors unless they have a special non-slip backing (you can buy this by the metre and sew it on to your existing rugs)

....

TIP

When decorating you'll need to take down the pictures on your walls. Before you do so draw a plan of the hanging pattern, noting what was where, so you'll be able to recreate the same arrangement on your bright, fresh, new walls

....

TIP

Old towels and bedlinen can be kept for dust sheets when decorating, or torn up for use as cleaning cloths

....

BATHROOM BASICS

Attractively decorated and filled with plants that thrive in a warm, moist atmosphere, the bathroom can be a little haven of peace. It should, of course, also be serviceable, easy to clean and well lit for shaving and putting on make-up.

No one wants to run out of the bathroom with dripping wet hair searching for clean towels or from the toilet because there is no loo roll. BE PREPARED: remember to replace stocks before they run out.

- keep your medicine cupboard and linen cupboard in perfect order. That way you'll never be desperately fumbling for a bathmat or an Alka-Seltzer in a hurry – if you have the space, buy in bulk
- if logistically possible, store back-up items behind or near the items they'll replace
- always make sure you have at least one, preferably two, spare packages of essential items such as these (since everybody's requirements are slightly different, adapt this list to suit yourself):
    o air fresheners

- o antiseptic
- o bath foam/gel/salts
- o bath cleaner
- o cotton buds
- o cotton wool
- o dental floss
- o deodorant
- o ear swabs
- o emery boards
- o eye make-up remover
- o hand cream
- o lavatory cleaner
- o make-up remover
- o moisturiser
- o nail varnish remover
- o plasters
- o razor/razor blades
- o shampoo
- o soap
- o talc
- o tampons
- o tissues
- o toilet rolls
- o toothbrushes
- o toothpaste

This running list can be compiled either in your bathroom on a pad for the purpose, or on your kitchen pegboard.

Safety in the bathroom

- keep all medicines and cleaning products out of children's reach
- don't use slippery polish on bathroom floors
- mop up immediately any water spilt on uncarpeted bathroom floors

- have a rubber mat in the bath. A grab handle is also useful for the very young and the very old
- when running children's baths, put cold water in first in case they fall in and scald themselves
- don't leave children in the bathroom alone
- don't use any electrical equipment other than a shaver (in a proper shaver socket) or a wall-mounted heater
- always have pull cords, not switches, for lights and heaters
- in case of burst pipes or overflow, don't leave plugs in baths or basins

....

TIP

Clean the bath daily – that way the tide mark won't get a chance to put in an appearance. Better still, train your family to clean the bath after they use it! Work is always halved when you DO IT NOW

....

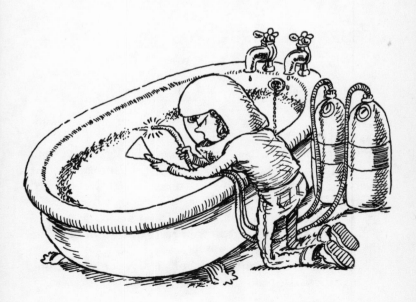

TIP

Keep your make-up brushes standing up in a large yoghurt pot or mug

TIP

Keep pump-action hand cream near every sink and basin in the house – then it becomes second nature to keep your hands soft

TIP

Don't keep lipsticks and eye make-up that were fashionable years ago. But do keep two different shades of foundations – for summer and winter, because your complexion is likely to be paler in winter, tanned in summer. Also keep a light moisturiser for summer and a richer one to deal with the harsh winds and central heating of winter. But don't have both out gathering dust at the same time

ESSENTIAL CUPBOARDS

Linen cupboard

Neatness is the essence of an organised linen cupboard and, as with bookshelves, there is more than one way to achieve this. You may like to arrange the contents by colour, item or size. But, whichever way you choose, get it tidy before it gets out of control. It only needs one sheet or towel dragged from the bottom of the pile and everything's in a mess.

- to keep the cupboard looking attractive, as well as tidy, place your towels in rolls instead of stacking them
- keep every component of a set (e.g. matching pillowcases and sheets) together

- place the folded side of towels etc. facing you – this enables you to extract only what you need, without pulling out other items as well

....

TIP

Consider storing spare toilet rolls, tissues and tampons in the base of the linen cupboard to make use of the floor space

....

Medicine cupboard

If, like most people's, your bathroom medicine cupboard is bulging, deal with it. DO IT NOW

- get rid of all your old medicines by taking them back to any chemist. Don't stockpile remedies

- the same goes for any medicine past its expiry date
- store medicine in a box such as a first aid kit high enough to be out of children's reach
- put everything you can into containers, by category (e.g. all hair stuff in one container, all bath salts and oils in another)
- put any complimentary miniature shampoos, hand creams etc. in round plastic cotton bud containers – one category in each
- if you take pills on a daily basis, and you work away from home, each night get out what you need for the next day and put them in your handbag – that way you won't ever be caught without them
- if regular pills are running low, get a new prescription from the doctor
- dispose of any medicine if its label has come off – don't take chances

....

TIP
Never take pills in the dark – you might muddle the containers and the results could be disastrous
....

3 | The Nine to Five Syndrome – Planning Ahead for the Working Day at Home or in the Office

Everyone 'works' at something. The mother of three under-fives 'works' just as much as the executive rushing from one business meeting to the next. And everyone has 'business' to deal with, too. Paying the insurance premiums and getting the car relicensed – and keeping proper records – are relatively just as important to the average family as signing a contract or buying an oil well might be to Someone in the City. So don't skip this chapter just because you commute to the supermarket rather than to an office. There's something useful here for everybody.

Management of your time in the office or at home can be summed up in four lines:

- I must do today
- I must delegate today
- I can postpone this today
- I must follow up today

If this sounds rather high-flown, remember that delegating something need be no more than asking your teenage son to clean the car for some extra pocket money, and following up can mean chasing that builder whose estimate should have arrived by now but hasn't.

SPLIT LIVES CAN RUN SMOOTHLY

Working at a job outside the home undoubtedly means you need to be even better organised if you're going to avoid unnecessary hassle in your life. You'll be in different places at fixed times and on fixed days, for starters, so you may have to use shops, hairdressers and cleaners near your place of work. And you'll need certain kinds of information and everyday equipment in duplicate, so you've always got it with you wherever you are.

Let's see just how good you are at dealing with this potential problem situation:

- can you go out straight from work knowing you've got all the things you need for the evening ahead?
- can you get back home and make a meal without going to the corner shop to pick something up?
- do you always remember to collect your dry cleaning and shoe repairs?

If you can't/don't, this chapter is for you.

USE YOUR WEEKENDS EFFECTIVELY

Weekends are when you'll want to relax, forget the strain of the workplace and enjoy life with family and friends. But with careful planning you can give up just a small part of your weekend and make the other 5 days run much more smoothly:

At weekends:
- cook for the week ahead – make casseroles and put them in the fridge, or freeze other dishes and prepared vegetables
- alternatively, budget for eating out or buying ready-made meals that you can pop in the microwave (NB

doing your own is likely to be healthier as well as cheaper!)

- make lunchtime sandwiches for yourself and/or the children for the week ahead, and freeze them

Every morning:

- remove from the freezer anything that's needed for that night's meal, and place it in the fridge to defrost

INFORMATION AT YOUR FINGERTIPS – WHEREVER YOU ARE

If you work, you'll need a diary (the biggest size that fits comfortably into your handbag, since you may not always want to keep it in your larger briefcase) or a Filofax. It may

SHE'S SO HIGH-POWERED SHE KEEPS HER HANDBAG IN HER DIARY.

seem a bore, but to make life easier in the long run you need to

- keep your diary as a straight copy of the diary chart in your kitchen at home
- compare the two at least every weekend, and preferably every evening, to make sure you're always up-to-date

This is the kind of information you'll find just as useful to have available at work as at home, to enable you to plan and buy ahead:

- birthdays of family and friends
- dates of everyone's next dental check-up
- TV licence renewal date

Make notes a week/month in advance, as appropriate, for items like:

- getting the car relicensed and MOTd – to avoid a rush to get it done at the last minute before the old one expires
- paying insurance premiums and making other large regular payments – so you can make sure there's enough money in the bank to cover your cheque/ standing order/direct debit
- approximate date when you'll next need to visit your hairdresser – that way you'll get the day, time and stylist you want

Your diary should also contain essential data such as

- passport number
- national insurance number
- private health scheme details
- bank account number
- bank sorting code
- details of building society accounts
- premium bond numbers

You'll probably be able to name lots more things that relate to the way you live. Good! That means you're already beginning to think carefully about the different elements in your day-to-day life – and that's the first step to PLANNING AHEAD.

BRIEFCASE NEATNESS

- keep papers, documents and stationery in one section and toiletries in another
- clear plastic folders take minimal space and are indispensable for grouping papers, especially if your briefcase doesn't have lots of separate compartments
- clear out your briefcase regularly – there's no point in wasting energy carting around a load of rubbish
- clean it from time to time with shoe cream – colourless so that any residue won't stain your clothes

Briefcase checklist

Your briefcase is not intended to be used as a suitcase! Nevertheless it won't be fulfilling its proper function if it doesn't contain certain essential items. How many of these are in your briefcase now?

- large lined pad
- pens (preferably at least two colours)
- pencil
- eraser
- ruler
- highlighter pens
- calculator
- address book ⎫
- diary ⎬ or Filofax
- week-at-a-glance programme
- dictating machine (if you use one)
- plastic folders

- stamps
- writing paper
- envelopes
- spare tights
- tissues
- moist tissues
- tampons
- aspirins or similar
- plasters
- needle and thread
- small scissors
- telescopic umbrella

YOUR HOME IS A WORKPLACE TOO

We've all heard the architect Le Corbusier's famous dictum that 'a house is a machine for living in'. Obviously it's much more than that, but to an extent he was right. If in your home you follow certain basic routines that are second nature in any well-organised office, life will be much simpler and you will seem effortlessly efficient!

- keep telephone and code books by the telephone (or in an agreed handy place if your phone is cordless). No one moves them!
- keep paper and pens by the telephone for message-taking
- in your kitchen or other convenient place keep a filing box (see below for more hints on filing) sub-divided into sections for
  - receipts
  - guarantees
  - cleaning instructions
  - any other categories you need

- cut out interesting newspaper articles (don't keep the whole paper, but note which paper it was, and the date) and file articles in clearly labelled folders which you then keep in a filing drawer
- keep a drawerful of greetings cards with no words printed inside – they can be used for birthdays, anniversaries, thank you notes or whatever
- write thank you letters immediately after the event
- write back to a friend within a week of receiving his or her letter, otherwise you'll never get round to doing it
- use as many 'desk-top' stationery items as you find helpful, e.g.
  - clear plastic folders for filing papers
  - Post-Its for sticking reminders on things
  - staples for keeping small papers together (paper clips fall off)
  - highlighter pens to pick out an important piece of information in e.g. newspaper articles
- have regular weeding-out sessions on all files, and throw away material no longer required
- keep a small watering can near your sink so it becomes routine to water your plants before leaving for work or starting other daily jobs

DON'T PILE – FILE!

A simple filing box such as can be bought at branches of W.H. Smith's or Ryman's will be quite adequate for many people's domestic paperwork. But in an office, or if you have a lot of documents to deal with at home, you may need further methods of organising your files. Whatever you choose, remember that the aim is to be able to find what you want immediately, without lengthy thought or searching. Make sure you don't devise a system that's too complex and thus defeats its own ends.

Consider filing in one or a number of these ways:

- alphabetically
- colour-coded by subject
- chronologically

Here's an example to show you how this works. Let's suppose you've decided to go for colour-coding by subject, and that you've chosen blue (a blue folder, or a blue tab) for your personal files. So you'll have a number of these blue files all appearing in alphabetical order, e.g.

- anniversaries
- birthdays
- children
- dates to remember
- gifts
- hairdresser
- knitting patterns
- lunch dates
- monthly budget

and interspersed with others – colour-coded perhaps pink for tax, orange for insurance and so on – within the general alphabetical order. Keep a list of all the files within each subject area, so you can go straight to what you want.

....

TIP

If there is any ambiguity about which file something goes in, put it in one file and cross-reference it from other relevant ones (e.g. put your car insurance policy in your car file, but cross-reference it from your insurance file)

....

TIP

Attach a Post-It to each piece of paper as it arrives – e.g. 'Pay by 20th', 'Ring for more details', 'Follow up at end December'

....

TIP

Change of address cards are small and get lost easily. Whenever you recieve one update your address book/ Filofax instantly

TIP

Keep a follow-up file containing all papers that need follow-up attention. Before you file, attach to each document a Post-It saying when you must follow up, and file them in this order. Make a habit of looking in this file every day

TIP

Make a copy of every letter you send (except perhaps social ones) and document. Use carbons for cheapness on the letters you write, yourself and have other documents Xeroxed at a copy shop. Copies save you endless trouble if you have to prove a point later

TIP

Running out of stamps is a nuisance but can be avoided. Little books are fine for your handbag but for business use (home or office) buy sheets or half-sheets so you can see at a glance how many you have. If the postage rates go up buy the equivalent number of 1p stamps to use up what's left. Alternatively just buy the stamps marked 1st class and 2nd class

GET ME TO THE OFFICE ON TIME

Getting to work is no fun for most of us – but crowded public transport and ill-tempered traffic snarl-ups seem even worse if you find you've run out of the house without that vital file for an important meeting. Here are some tips for making your mornings as trouble-free as possible:

- before you go to bed, park everything you'll need for

the day ahead right by the front door – if you can't get out without moving your briefcase or umbrella you're more likely to take them with you

- the same applies to letters for posting
- if a colleague asks you to bring in something special the next day, find it immediately and again park it by the front door
- if you go on working during the evening once you've got home, make sure all files etc. are returned to your briefcase as soon as you've finished
- to remind yourself about items that can't be packed up the night before, like your lunchtime sandwiches, stick a Post-It on the front door – if you can't open the door without lifting that label you're unlikely to end up lunchless!

ONCE YOU'VE GOT TO WORK

- keep in your desk drawers useful items such as
  - tampons
  - hand cream
  - toothbrush and toothpaste
  - umbrella
  - anything else from the briefcase checklist above that you might need during the course of the working day
- if you lunch with clients or have evening meetings (particularly if you do so with little or no warning) always keep some spare, clean, smart clothes and shoes in the office
- if you suffer from PMT, try not to fix meetings, especially important ones, during likely difficult days

....

TIP
'A place for everything and everything in its place' sounds horribly schoolmarm-ish, doesn't it? But it works! If you always put your season ticket into the same pocket in your bag, and if you always put your diary back in your briefcase when you've consulted it, you'll never be caught out. This is true of practically everything in both the home and office. DO IT NOW

....

4 | Pay Those Bills – Organising Your Finances

Who manages the money in your home? Women tend to take on at least the domestic side of financial affairs, but whatever the division of responsibility in your household the important thing is to keep yourself informed and up-to-date. Money matters need hold no fears for you if you act sensibly and PLAN AHEAD.

HOW TO BUDGET PAINLESSLY

'Annual income twenty pounds, annual expenditure nineteen nineteen six, result happiness. Annual income twenty pounds, annual expenditure twenty pounds ought and six, result misery.' So said Mr Micawber – and he was right. Budgeting is really not difficult, and can even be enjoyable once you find yourself mastering your finances instead of the other way round.

It's a two-stage process to set up. First, here's an easy-to-follow, step-by-step guide to drawing up a plan of your annual expenditure:

1. Write down what you earn net each year – i.e. after tax, national insurance, pension contributions and any other deductions.

2. Write down your essential annual expenses for the family. These are probably made up of most or all of the following:

£

- mortgage or rent
- electricity
- gas
- community charge
- water rates
- telephone
- TV licence
- bus pass/rail season ticket
- insurance premiums
- hire purchase repayments
- car: insurance, petrol, road fund licence
- credit card and store card bills
- membership subscriptions
- school fees
- essential clothing
- food and other essential household shopping

Sub-total

Now add in reasonable allowances for the following. Some are clearly more important than others, so SORT OUT YOUR PRIORITIES.

£

- presents
- postage/stationery
- dry cleaning
- dentist/optician/doctor's prescriptions
- vet
- hairdresser
- non-essential clothes
- cinema/theatre/video hire
- travel
- holidays

- Christmas
- plants/flowers for the house
- eating out/pub
- entertaining at home
- make-up/perfume
- garden (seeds, bulbs, plants, tools)
- DIY equipment and materials
- hobbies
- evening classes
- books
- stocking drinks cabinet
- cigarettes

Sub-total _____

Grand total _____

Add up all the items on your list of expenditure and take the total away from your net income. Any surplus should be invested to earn interest (more on this later in the chapter).

The next stage is to write down on your kitchen diary chart (or on a separate chart if you find that easier) exactly when these payments have to be made (wherever it's possible to pin them down that closely and the approximate date each month when your salary is safely in the bank. If you are paid weekly, adjust accordingly. The aim is to have money available in the right place to pay those bills at the right time.

What you've now got is the basis of a simple cash flow system. If you don't want to be bothered with this stage of the process, the bank will do it for you if you open a budget account (see below).

To make this system really work for you from year to year there's also a third stage. For this you need to keep a clear record of all the payments you *do* actually make in the various categories, so that at the end of the year you can see how accurate your budget was. If you've over-spent, you may need to cut down on some of those non-essentials the following year. If you've under-spent, treat yourself to a bottle of champagne or award yourself some extra holiday spending money.

PAY IT NOW?

Many people say it's sound business sense not to pay a bill until the last reminder. Why let someone else earn interest on your money? Personally I don't recommend that because the object of being organised (and indeed the idea behind this book) is to free your mind from clutter by DOING IT NOW.

Nevertheless some people will quite understandably want to make a compromise. It's easy to pay bills immediately if you have a good salary but are pressed for time, less so if you're a pensioner whose job is making ends meet. So let's be reasonable and say that there are really only two ways of settling your bills:

- pay it now
- work out in advance when would be the best time for you to pay

The last is not difficult if you keep the budget details mentioned above and note the date by which each bill has to be paid (taking into account possible postal and bank clearing delays for items like credit card bills).

DIFFERENT METHODS OF PAYMENT

Standing orders

This is how most people pay their mortgage. You complete a form instructing the bank to make, on your behalf, regular monthly payments to the building society. The monthly amounts can only be altered on your instructions.

Direct debit

This is a form of payment which is sometimes requested, or insisted on, when the sum payable varies. As with a standing order, you fill out a form instructing the bank to make payments on your behalf. You should receive prior notification when the amount of the payment changes.

Budget accounts

You may like to consider opening a budget account. To do so, you present the bank with a breakdown of your annual expenditure like we've just done. You then pay into your account a mutually agreed sum in regular monthly instalments, in return for which the bank guarantees to pay your bills as and when they come in. This is particularly useful if you don't have a *regular* income (e.g. if you are paid fees rather than a salary).

SPREADING THE BURDEN OF THOSE ESSENTIAL PAYMENTS

- the community charge can be paid to your local authority in instalments by standing order, or you can send or take a cheque to the town hall
- water rates are paid in the same way, but in eight monthly instalments
- telephone bills must be paid in full – there are no monthly instalment arrangements. To help, you can

buy savings stamps from British Telecom or at any post office

- gas and electricity bills can be paid via a budget account (don't confuse this with a budget account at the bank) which is estimated on a monthly basis by the electricity and gas boards. Alternatively you can buy stamps at their showrooms
- TV licences can be paid either by special stamps from the post office or in equal monthly instalments

But it *doesn't* always *pay to spread the cost*

- pay your road fund licence annually, because to pay six-monthly costs you more
- if you can afford it in the first place, buy an annual season ticket rather than weekly/monthly/quarterly. It will be cheaper in the end
- private medical scheme payments can be made monthly

CHECK THOSE CHEQUES

- it's essential to check your monthly bank statements. Mistakes can and do happen. Make time to go through each item carefully against your own records (see below)
- enter in your paying-in book accurate details of money paid in (amount/cheque number/source/date paid in)
- keep all slips from cash dispensers until you've had the statement that covers them
- it's useful to enter all transactions (cheques written/ deposits made/withdrawals from cash dispensers) on

the stubs in your chequebook. This provides back-up records and has the advantage of everything being in one place

BANKING ON YOUR BUILDING SOCIETY

Now that building societies have gone into banking you may prefer to write cheques on this kind of account (you get interest – see below) rather than a bank account. But remember:

- building society passbooks don't print all details of deposits, so you must keep your own records of the source of each cheque paid in
- some building society accounts have dispensed with passbooks and use only plastic cards. In this case it is essential to write down full details yourself

KEEPING YOUR CREDITWORTHINESS

- keep all your credit card and store card vouchers until the sums appear on your statement. When you've checked them off you can throw the vouchers away
- while you're still keeping them don't let these vouchers clutter up your wallet or handbag – clip them into separate piles relating to each card, and keep them tidily in a plastic folder
- before you file the vouchers, see if any bear the annoying legend 'goods' and write on them what you actually bought. Otherwise in a month's time, when your statement comes, you'll have completely forgotten what the 'goods' were

....
TIP
Keep at home a list of all your credit card and store card numbers, together with the phone number to ring if you lose one or have it stolen. The quicker you report a lost card the less financial responsibility you may have to bear if a thief takes your card on a shopping spree!
....

GETTING TO THE INTERESTING PART

Organised people make the most of their money. Put any salary that's not spoken for into a sensible investment like a building society account, but remember there are a few disadvantages about those exciting-sounding high-interest accounts:

- they often require a large sum to be invested, and if the balance falls below that sum you get a lower rate of interest

- you may not be able to get your money out quickly (if the washing machine packs up, do you really want to wait 3 months to get at your savings?)
- they don't all pay a guaranteed higher rate of interest. You'll feel pretty sick if you lock your money up for 3 months or more and then find the rate drops after a week or two!

Many building societies now offer banking facilities with a chequebook, and many banks are offering current accounts that pay interest. It's worth spending a little time shopping around and comparing rates of interest/facilities available/accessibility of your money and so on. Be organised – do the best you can with your hard-earned money, so you can enjoy the rewards you deserve in due course!

TAX AFFAIRS

Everyone hates filling out their tax returns. Here are a few tips for making that annual chore less of a pain:

- at the end of the tax year (April) your employer should give you a form P60, stating how much you have earned and how much tax you have paid in the previous tax year. Keep it in a safe place (the best place is a folder or file marked Tax)
- if your mortgage is under £30,000, your tax relief is given to you automatically under the MIRAS scheme. If it's more than that, you have to get from your building society a statement of the amount you've paid in the preceding tax year. Make sure you get one, and keep it in a safe place
- building society account interest has to be entered on your tax return in case you're liable for higher rate tax (basic rate tax is paid by the building society on your

behalf). If you have a passbook your interest payments will have been entered on one of your visits to your local branch. If there's no passbook, you must obtain from the head office a statement of interest paid. Keep it in a safe place

- remember also to enter on your tax return any benefits provided by your employer that may be taxable (e.g. car, clothes allowance, season ticket loan)
- keep all receipts for subscriptions that are allowable against tax (e.g. trade union membership)
- do read carefully through the guide that accompanies your annual tax return when you receive it. Don't toss it in the bin – you may find it surprisingly helpful
- as with all unpleasant chores, the thinking about it is often the worst part. When the envelope from the tax man lands on your doormat, DO IT NOW

WASTE NOT, WANT NOT

Finally, for those on a limited budget, here are some helpful hints to make sure your money goes where it's needed, and isn't wasted.

- insulate to save on heating bills
- change to a lower-wattage or long-life bulb in places that don't matter too much (e.g. the loo – but don't cut down on light in the kitchen or on the stairs)
- don't half-fill the washing machine and then run it on a full-load programme
- defrost your fridge and freezer regularly so they don't use more electricity than necessary
- use the oven sensibly (e.g. bake two cakes together and freeze one of them)

- buy food for the freezer in bulk if you can afford to. It saves money in the long run
- choose basic clothes that will mix and match cleverly, and jazz them up with colourful accessories
- whenever possible, make social phone calls during the cheap rate (6 p.m. to 8 p.m. Monday to Friday, and all day Saturday and Sunday)
- give up smoking – you'll feel better, too!
- don't try and prepare a budget for yourself that's so complicated that you give up. DON'T AIM FOR PERFECTION. The aim of this book is to *help* you, not to make life more difficult!

5 | Filing Your Clothes – How to Organise Your Wardrobe

Why is it some people always look 'together' and others just look a mess? Organisation is the answer. Being organised with your clothes means BEING PREPARED when it comes to shopping, laundering, dry cleaning and putting away – whether you've got masses of clothes or only very few.

SHOPPING EFFECTIVELY

- when clothes-shopping alone for your family, take their measurements with you:
  - children's chest sizes and lengths
  - men's chest, neck and sock sizes. This will save you from becoming a yo-yo. Why not keep this information in your diary or Filofax so you've always got it with you – then all those impulse buys will at least fit!
- if you're looking for, say, a sweater to match a skirt you've already got, don't rely on memory but take the skirt with you
- if shopping for shoes in the summer when you're not wearing tights, take a pair of pop sox with you

LAUNDERING AND DRY CLEANING

- launder and dry clean frequently – ground-in dirt and stains are much harder to remove
- keep a range of stain removers handy for 'first aid' to clothes – we all have accidents
- remember that 'biological' stains (egg, blood, grass etc.) respond best to cold water. Hot water sets the stain
- make your dry cleaner's life easier by telling them what the stains on your clothes are – if you know
- follow care instructions on clothing labels – if you machine-wash something that says hand-wash or dry clean only you shouldn't be surprised if it shrinks or the colours run!

- before putting clothes into the washing machine remove all belts and unwashable trimmings. Check all pockets – well-laundered tissues and sweets are a pain to remove later!
- repair torn hems, replace missing buttons etc. as soon as you notice them. DO IT NOW
- keep your skirts immaculate by pressing after wearing and before putting away

....

TIP
To stop stuff snarling up in the washing machine, tie all belts and fasten buttons and zips. If you wash your tights in the machine, put them in a special laundry bag made for the purpose
....

SHOESHINE SENSE

- clean boots and shoes often – that way you can always do the job quickly
- brush mud and dirt off shoes (wait until it's dry) before you polish
- using colourless polish or shoe cream will prevent unwanted stains on your clothes while you're shoe-cleaning – keep tins of cover-up polish such as Tuxan for occasional bad scuffs and scratches
- before wearing new shoes for the first time give them a coat of colourless polish for protection, and if the soles and/or heels are smooth and slippery scratch them with an old fork
- clean fabric shoes by first dusting them and then washing off the dirt with soapy water and a nailbrush. Alternatively use a spray-on fabric shampoo

- clean everyday dust and dirt off suede shoes frequently with a special suede brush, used dry. Shampoo them occasionally with an easy-to-use spray-on suede cleaner
- get boots and shoes repaired (especially heels) before they're completely worn down
- don't break down the backs of your shoes when you put them on – use a shoe horn to ease your foot in
- spray winter boots with a silicone water-repellent to keep them reasonably waterproof

....

TIP

If your shoe polish has gone all dry and caked, stir a spoonful of paraffin into it

....

TIP

Keep shoe cleaning equipment handy in the kitchen so it becomes a daily twenty-second routine before going to work

....

WARDROBE WISDOM

The main reason why people have cluttered closets is that they keep far too much. Let's see just how bad a state your clothes are in by answering the following questions!

	No	Yes
1. Is there anything in your clothes cupboards or drawers which you've not worn for over a year?		
2. Is there anything which you bought at a sale and have never worn?		

3. Are there any items which you are 'going to give away . . . soon'?

4. Are there any clothes which you 'might keep after they've been altered'?

5. Are there any garments which are too small, but which 'will fit after I've lost weight'?

6. Have you kept anything 'just in case it comes back into fashion'?

7. Have you kept anything 'because it might be useful one day'?

If you answered yes to more than three, you're guilty of keeping cluttered closets. But don't worry – help is at hand! If you don't want your closet to look like a junk heap, be ruthless. Follow my rule of thumb: don't keep anything which you haven't worn for a year. (There are a few exceptions, of course: you wouldn't want to throw out your sheepskin jacket because last winter was mild, or a pretty sundress that you didn't wear because it rained all summer. Just use your common sense – and whatever you decide to throw out, DO IT NOW.)

So let's assume that, like most people, you've got a bursting-at-the-seams, disordered clothes closet and you need a bit of guidance to deal with it. Here's how to sort and then either discard or rearrange your clothes:

- take out each garment singly
- consider its suitability/wearability (don't rationalise, don't keep 'just in case' – be ruthless)

Now make four piles:

- keep just as they are
  - o wash/iron/send to cleaners
  - o repair/alter
  - o discard

Clothes for keeping

Put these back in the wardrobe – for the moment only. We'll come on to proper organisation of what you *do* keep in a page or two.

Clothes for washing/ironing/going to the cleaners

Put washable garments into the machine or hand-wash them if appropriate. Dry and iron them as soon as possible – don't leave them lying about half-done. If they need dry cleaning rather than washing, put them in the boot of your car and be sure to drop them off at the cleaners.

Clothes for repair

Put these into a plastic bin bag and label it. If you're doing the repairs yourself, put the bag next to your sewing machine or sewing basket, and make sure you get down to it later that day. If the repairs are going to be done by someone else, or at the cleaners, put the bag in the boot of the car ready to be dropped off as soon as possible.

Clothes for discarding

Put them in a plastic bin bag and label it. Then arrange for them to be collected, or put them in the boot of your car ready to drop them at a local charity shop. DO IT NOW.

....

TIP
When ironing, learn to SORT OUT YOUR PRIORITIES. Providing enough clean shirts/blouses for the week ahead is far more important than ironing underwear or tea towels
....

Quick hints for trouble-free dressing

- after wearing, never put back clothes which need either cleaning or repairing – nothing's more annoying than getting out a garment, only to discover a paint mark or missing buttons
- each night get out your clothes for the next day – not just the jacket and skirt, but the accompanying blouse, shoes, bag, belt, jewellery and underwear. This way you can see at a glance if anything is missing, and you can BE PREPARED

The clothes closet as filing cabinet

Now we're ready to turn again to the garments you've decided to keep. Just like the papers in your office, or the tins in your kitchen cupboard, your clothes should be arranged – filed, really – in an organised fashion.

There are lots of ways of filing clothes. I find a very

sensible way to start for practically everyone is to divide them first by season, then by colour or colour co-ordination. In other words, however small your closets, they should be divided into two. Some clothes, such as blouses, work for all seasons – just move these across to the relevant half of your closet when you go from one season to the next. How you go on depends on your lifestyle and the quantity of clothes you own. Here are a few suggestions.

If you have loads of clothes and go to a lot of functions:
- divide into day/evening
- then sub-divide into smart/casual
- then sub-divide again into suits/skirts and jackets/blouses/dresses/trousers
- now file the garments according to colour

If you have fewer clothes and don't have a hectic social life you might like simply to:
- divide first by type of garment
- then sub-divide by colour

If your body weight fluctuates, an easier way might be to:
- divide into smaller/larger sizes
- or divide into looser/more fitting garments

If you lead a particular lifestyle or do a job that requires a certain type of clothing (e.g. barristers need dark clothes, and teachers want something tough and serviceable) you may want to:
- divide first into working 'uniform' and other garments

If you go to the kind of functions where hats are worn (and have lots of wardrobe space) you might want to:
- put colour-matching and co-ordinating hats (and indeed shoes) near the garments you would wear them with

Take a piece of paper and work out your own scheme, using these ideas as a starting point and taking into account the nature of your working day and social life, the amount of clothes you possess and the number and capacity of your closets, drawers etc. Not everyone is lucky enough to have the space (or money) for serried ranks of beautifully fitted wardrobes. Just do the best you can with what you've got, and be prepared to experiment a bit until you end up with something that really works for you. And remember, it won't work unless you put your clothes back in the right condition, in the right place and at the right time. It'll be worth it – you'll save endless frustration, embarrassment and time if your clothes are properly organised.

....

TIP
Try and find somewhere (bedroom/landing/hall) for a full-length mirror. It will tell you straightaway if a

garment looks terrible on you or if your hemline is drooping. Get into the habit of looking in it every day – front, sides and back – before you leave the house

....
TIP
Use wooden, plastic or padded fabric coathangers, not wire ones which get mis-shapen and rusty. Don't waste good clothes on broken-down old hangers – decent ones are a sensible investment
....

Hang those accessories

- keep your favourite accessories within easiest reach inside your closets. Hang belts and men's ties on the inside of the door
- if you haven't got room in your closet for your belts, an attractive alternative is to store them in a straw basket
- jewellery is good pinned to a pegboard with hooks, provided you wear it regularly so it doesn't get a chance to gather dust. Items that are worn only occasionally, like long sparkly evening ear-rings, should be put away where they won't attract dust and dirt

....
TIP
Let air circulate in your closets – if you don't, your clothes will lose their freshness and become targets for moths
....

Storing boots and shoes

- keep your shoes in shape – put shoe trees in as soon as you take them off, i.e. when they're still soft and warm

- if you've got the space, store your shoes and boots in their original boxes, which keeps them dust-free. The other alternative – on shoe racks at the bottom of your closet – isn't quite as dust-free
- air shoes and boots thoroughly before putting them away until the next summer/winter season

A BASIC WARDROBE ON A BUDGET

If you go for a few good, well-cut, basic garments in easy-to-coordinate shades, and use accessories to provide brighter colour, interest and variety, you should find:

- your main garments are wearable longer
- you're less inclined to impulse/panic buy
- your closets don't clog up

Suit

A good suit can be the key item in a working woman's wardrobe – the perfect answer to many social and business functions. Choose a classic style in a plain colour that can be worn year in and year out, dressed up or down as necessary, and worn with a cool blouse in summer or with a sweater and coat in winter. Recently fashion has favoured suits with co-ordinating rather than matching skirts and jackets – whichever you choose, remember that the better the cloth and cut, the longer it will last and the smarter it will look.

Coat

This is the item you should spend the most money on – get the best quality you can afford. Lucky you if you can afford a new coat every year and can follow fashion detail and colour! If you can't, choose a classic style in a basic colour (navy, black, camel, grey, brown). Make sure your coat covers all day-dress lengths in your wardrobe and is in any case long enough to keep you warm in the depths of winter. Fashion elements such as shawls, scarves and boots will ring the changes on this essential basic garment.

Raincoat

This is the most-used item in most English people's wardrobe. If you can't afford a winter coat as well, buy a raincoat with a detachable warm lining (or buy a warm lining separately). Darker colours are the most serviceable ones because they don't need to go to the cleaners so often. If your raincoat says it is washable by all means pop it in the machine, but remember it will need to be reproofed afterwards (you can do it yourself with a special silicone spray).

Skirts and trousers

Here again, particularly for winter wear, choose the best fabric and cut you can afford. A couple of pairs of each garment should be enough to enable you to mix and match cleverly. Most useful again would be a dark colour. Choose classic styles which won't date.

Shirts and blouses

Classic, again, is the name of the game. Create variety with scarves and jewellery. Make sure your shirts are always clean and crisply ironed. If ironing is a problem, go for uncrushable synthetics. Try to have three – one to wear, one in the wash and one spare.

Knitwear

Choose wool, lambswool or (if you can afford it) cashmere for wearability, washability, fit and warmth. Synthetics may be cheaper (though not always) and can be machine washed, but they have a tendency to 'pill' and they go out of shape. Buy one or two fun jumpers or cardigans as well if you can, and a long cardigan is very useful to wear over a dress, skirt or trousers, particularly on cool summer evenings.

Evening wear

Buy yourself a long skirt in velvet or taffeta – choose plain black or another rich, dark colour such as midnight blue, dark green or maroon. Vary the look with as many different tops as you feel your social life warrants – they can range from an elegant long-sleeved silk blouse for formal dinners to something sexy and strappy for summer parties. Vary your jewellery too, but you'll only need one little evening bag to go with the skirt.

....
TIP
Keep your knitwear in perfect condition by hand-washing them in cool water and a specially formulated liquid such as Woolite. Never let them get too dirty. After rinsing, roll them in a towel to absorb excess water and then dry flat, away from heat. When dry, press with a medium iron over a clean damp cloth.
....
TIP
To beat the moth menace, keep all knitwear and fine wool scarves in firmly sealed polythene bags.
....

Accessories

Always buy classic bags and shoes unless you have enough money to be adventurous in style and colours. A large leather handbag is usually the most efficient and durable for everyday use. Bags for evening wear can be smaller and more frivolous.

Even if your basic everyday bag isn't one of the 'organiser' kind, kitted out with loads of compartments and hidey-holes, it's bound to have at least one pocket. I suggest you put into this your

- keys
- bus pass/season ticket
- wallet

- chequebook
- pen
- credit cards

In the body of the bag go your
- diary/Filofax
- notebook
- cheque card (must be kept separate from chequebook)
- card with details of next of kin, home and work phone numbers etc. in case of accident
- make-up bag (keep in here a few extras such as plasters, tampons, aspirins and safety pins)
- comb (and brush if your hair is long and/or wilful)
- gloves
- tissues
- moist tissues
- spare tights
- train/bus timetable

You can have lots of fun with belts and scarves – just make sure your belts are large enough for you to wear comfortably (that includes sitting) without nasty rolls of surplus midriff appearing! Some people are very clever at tying silk and fine wool scarves round a coat, dress or blouse collar – if you want to add splashes of colour to an otherwise low-key classic outfit, this is the way to do it.

Don't forget a pair of basic colour leather gloves to complement your shoes and handbag, and some warm wool gloves or sheepskin mitts (both very reasonably priced).

6 | *Getting from* A *to* B

TAKE THE TRAUMA OUT OF TRAVEL

Whether you holiday in the UK or abroad, whether you go by car or fly, there are certain basic essentials that can make all the difference to your well-earned vacation. No one likes to arrive at their destination with all the wrong clothes, exhausted, fractious children and no supply of their regular pills. The same rules apply to business trips abroad, too. This scenario covers a wide spectrum of people, so I'll try and deal with all eventualities. Just pick out from my lists and handy hints those items that concern you, and your trips away from home should be doubly enjoyable and successful.

Planning ahead

Some things need to be thought about – and *done* – well in advance
- checking expiry dates on passports
- checking whether you need a visa
- getting any necessary vaccinations
- buying tickets
- booking your accommodation
- getting insurance
- ordering foreign currency/travellers' cheques

Travelling abroad by car

- do you need an international driving licence for the countries you're visiting (check with AA or RAC)?

- check rules for driving in the countries you're going to (again, consult AA or RAC). Do you need to buy:
  - a warning triangle
  - a petrol can
  - a kit to adjust your lights so they dip to the right?
  - a spare set of lamp bulbs?

....
TIP
If you're taking your car abroad, buy an up-to-date copy of the AA/RAC handbook on driving abroad. These books contain invaluable information on road signs, driving regulations, speed limits etc.
....

Insurance

Your insurance should cover at least
- accident
- illness
- cancellation
- loss of luggage

Shop around for the best deal and read all the small print – this kind of short-term insurance isn't usually very expensive, so go for the best rather than the cheapest. By saving a few pounds on a policy with a cheaper premium you might be storing up trouble for yourself if disaster does strike.

If you are going to an EC country, take also a copy of
- form E111

This is available from your local DSS office and gives you reciprocal arrangements to our own NHS scheme. The details vary from one country to another. Sometimes you pay nothing, sometimes you pay up-front and can recover the cost when you get back home, and there are all sorts of variations in between. Read the details for the countries you intend visiting before you go, so you know exactly what to do in the event of an emergency.

If travelling by car, write to your insurance company for a
- green card

They may say a green card is no longer necessary in EC countries. Wrong – or at any rate not quite accurate! A green card gives you the same cover as you've paid for in the UK – if you don't get a green card, on holiday you'll get no more than the minimum legal cover of the country concerned, which might only be third party.

Vaccination

Before visiting these countries some kind of vaccination is usually advisable, often mandatory:
- Barbados
- Brazil
- China
- Egypt
- Gambia
- Greece
- India
- Israel
- Jamaica
- Kenya
- Malaysia
- Morocco
- Seychelles
- Spain
- Thailand
- Tunisia

- Turkey
- Virgin Islands
- Yugoslavia

The sort of diseases you'll need to be immunised against include:
- cholera
- hepatitis A and B
- malaria
- polio
- tetanus
- tuberculosis
- typhoid
- yellow fever

Courses of malaria pills must be started well before you travel, so make enquiries several weeks ahead.

If in any doubt, check with your doctor. Remember, too, that local conditions and requirements may change from time to time, so it's always worth double-checking with the embassy/high commission of the countries concerned, to ensure that no new epidemic has broken out.

Finally, don't forget to
- take those vital vaccination certificates with you

You wouldn't want to be turned back at the frontier or – even worse – given an on-the-spot injection with a dubious hypodermic.

....

TIP
While you're away leave all your house plants out of direct sunlight in a cool room on trays, having watered them generously before leaving. Alternatively buy special self-watering appliances.

....

Pack up your troubles . . .

How to pack is an art form in itself, and we'll get on to that a little later. Meanwhile, here are a few memory joggers for those little essentials whose absence can spoil any holiday.

Remember to pack:

- passports
- tickets
- insurance documents
- E111
- private health insurance (BUPA, PPP etc.) document, if appropriate
- sunglasses
- sun filter cream
- sellotape (to secure tops on jars)
- ear plugs (in case of noisy bedrooms)
- eye mask – for peaceful sleep (and for the plane)
- travelling iron
- continental adaptor
- hair dryer
- door wedge (for added security on the inside of your bedroom door)
- note of all the family's clothing sizes in continental equivalents
- pocket dictionary in the language(s) of the countries you're visiting
- phrase book
- duplicate toilet bag which should also contain:
  - air/seasickness pills
  - the family's essential medicines
  - prescription for any long-term medicines (in case of emergency)
  - spare packet of contraceptive pills, if you take them
  - tampons

Tick off each item as it gets packed

PACKING CHECKLIST

Country of visit: (1) (2) (3)

Temperature during stay:

Length of stay:

Item	Daywear Item/Colour	Evening Item/Colour	Shoes Colour	Accessories Colour	Nightwear and Underwear	Toilet bag Items
Swimwear/ skiwear						
Jeans/trousers						
Shorts/culottes/ dungarees						
Skirts						
T-Shirts/blouses						
Dresses						
Sweaters/jackets cardigans/coat						
Packed in: which item of luggage						

- o nappies, cream etc. if you're travelling with a baby
- money in various forms (see below)

Money

Take with you
- enough local currency for when you first arrive
- travellers' cheques. Safety measures:
  - o note the cheque numbers as soon as you receive them – keep a note both at home and with your holiday luggage
  - o don't countersign cheques in advance
  - o keep the receipt for your cheques separate from the cheques themselves
  - o don't take all your cheques out with you at the same time
  - o try not to take them with you to the beach. Since hotel rooms are not necessarily secure either, ask to deposit them in the hotel safe
  - o when going out, put them at the bottom of your bag where they are more difficult for pickpockets to reach
- enough sterling for the day of your return

If you're travelling by air, all the above items go in your cabin baggage, along with
- suitcase keys
- change of clothes (especially underwear) in case of emergency

Remember, you can perfectly well spend a vacation in Greece while your luggage holidays in Paris or even stays at home in Heathrow. BE PREPARED!

If you're going by car, this bag of essential items goes next to you.

TIP
Take addressed self-adhesive labels for people to whom
you want to send cards. This way you won't forget anyone,
and you won't have to take your address book away with
you

How to get it all together

Now that I've shown you how to prepare in advance for
your holiday, here's a step-by-step guide for packing that
will enable you to arrive at the other end with creaseless
clothes.

First, a word about suitcases. The best type for most people is

- 26-inch or preferably 28-inch
- soft-topped (for expansion)
- with internal straps to keep everything in place
- with a zip all round plus straps over for double security
- with detachable wheels on the base
- with a detachable pulley handle on top

1. Get out all the clothes you intend packing and hang them on the wardrobe doors or on a rack if you have one.

2. Assemble all your old polythene clothes covers from the cleaners and some polythene food bags for smaller items. All your clothes and any small items that aren't stuffed inside shoes should ideally be polythene-covered.

3. Open your suitcase and first pack into it a carrier bag to put your wet swimsuits in, and a canvas-type bag in which to bring back souvenirs.

4. Next, pack a beach towel flat across the entire base of the case, making a flat surface on top of which you can pack the rest of your stuff.

....

TIP
Cut down on aching muscles and excess baggage costs. Buy small sizes of toiletries specially for holidays. Alternatively buy small plastic bottles and jars and fill them from your everyday larger sizes – but you *must* label them

....

TIP
Keep all your polythene covers from the cleaners – they're invaluable at packing time

....

5. Pack all your shoes, stuffing each with your knickers and bras, right into the toe section. Wrap each shoe in polythene to stop them rubbing together and scuffing, and pack the members of each pair toe to heel.

6. It's important to make sure that each layer is nice and flat – if you aren't taking enough shoes to cover the entire base of the case, fill the spaces with toiletries to the same depth.

7. Next come swimsuits and nightwear, and any jewellery you want to take, packed in the crevices.

8. After this comes your beach wrap, which will also double as a dressing gown. Fold it once only, so it fills the whole surface of the case.

....
TIP
Fold dresses and trousers only once. Don't fold skirts, shorts and shirts at all – just lay them full length along the case
....

9. Then pack heavier items like trousers and shorts. Put them all in on hangers and make sure you create a level surface.

10. Then come sweatshirts, sweaters and T-shirts, and then dresses.

....
TIP
Remember for Catholic and Moslem countries to take a headscarf and cardigan/long-sleeved shirt, plus a respectable knee-length skirt
....

11. On the very top you place delicate items such as silk shirts.

12. Put a final layer of polythene on top of everything.

13. Fasten the straps to secure everything inside, then close and lock the case, making sure it's clearly labelled with your name, home address and that of your destination.

....
TIP
Don't pack a sun hat – they're far too bulky. Buy one cheaply on holiday and throw it out when you go home. If you're going somewhere with a pebble beach, pack a pair of plastic shoes
....

You may like to adapt my step-by-step guide and checklist to suit your own particular requirements – if you have a baby, for instance, you'll want to compile a complete checklist of his or her clothes, equipment and food. Just remember certain basic, sensible rules:

- creases hate polythene!
- heaviest stuff goes nearest the bottom
- pack tightly so nothing moves en route
- pack each layer level

....
TIP
If you have a pet, book boarding kennels several months in advance and make sure you have an up-to-date vaccination certificate
....

Before you go

Don't forget to
- cancel the milk
- cancel the newspapers
- ask the post office to hold your post

Unfortunately this doesn't deal with the free newspapers and hand-delivered circulars we all get lumbered with – a dead giveaway to any burglar. So
- leave a key with a neighbour if possible (and don't forget to bring them a thank-you present)
- unplug all electrical appliances (except fridge/freezer)

Enjoy your flight

Be comfortably dressed for travel by air:
- wear a track suit or something equally loose and comfortable
- remember your feet swell on aircraft, so wear trainers or take slippers in your cabin baggage

....

TIP
If you have your fridge/freezer wired on a separate electrical circuit you can leave them on but turn everything else off at the mains
....

- wear wool or cotton socks and make sure you have a sweater with you in case the cabin gets cold
- alcohol and altitudes don't mix – stick to mineral water and fruit juice
- remember to take your travel sickness pills in good time if you need them
- eat lightly
- take small games, toys and books to keep kids

amused. A favourite teddy will help calm the worries of unfamiliar surroundings both on the plane and at the other end!

....

TIP
Mark your case with coloured stickers or luminous paint to help you recognise it on the carousel baggage claim
....

On your return

- try and have one spare day before you return to work, so you can catch up on all the accumulated chores and paperwork
- immediately restock used up items in things like toilet bags, so you're ready to travel again at a moment's notice
- add items to buy to the list on your kitchen pegboard

MOVING HOUSE

Some removal companies produce very useful checklists of their own. In case yours doesn't – and in any case for cross-checking – here are my tips for making what's meant to be one of the most traumatic events in our lives less of an agony!

Three weeks before you move

- cancel the milk (to be stopped the day you leave) and pay the bill
- deal the same way with the newspapers
- run the contents of your freezer down
- buy and send change of address cards to:
  - local authority (for rates)
  - water board (for water rates)
  - gas board
  - electricity board

and arrange with both for a final meter reading to be taken and the service disconnected at your old house, also reconnection and initial meter reading at your new home

  - DVLC (for your car)
  - all companies with whom you have insurance
  - doctor
  - dentist
  - optician
  - private health care scheme
  - inland revenue/accountant
  - credit card companies
  - bank
  - any stores where you have accounts
  - any clubs/other organisations to which you belong

  o any magazines etc. to which you subscribe
- arrange with the post office to redirect any mail that still comes to your old address. This saves you relying on the goodwill of the newcomers

Packing

- prepare a plan of the new house and number the rooms. Label each box and item of furniture with the corresponding number
- pack your clothes in suitcases
- pack all your china and glassware in two layers of newspapers – NB sometimes the removers insist on doing this themselves, or they won't insure you against breakages
- all your bedlinen can be packed in plastic clothes covers or bin liners
- don't forget to take your pets (or put them in kennels until you've settled in)
- pack what little frozen food you have left in an insulated cool-box. It should keep for about 8 hours
- pack house plants in cardboard boxes with newspaper stuffed round the pots to keep them firm and upright

GETTING THE BEST OUT OF YOUR WHEELS

Make your car work for you. You should be able to rely on it, and a few easy measures will ensure that you can.

....

TIP
Always lock your car even when leaving it for only a couple of minutes
....

Car care

It's in everyone's best interests to know a little about basic car maintenance.

- check the oil level regularly – say once a week – by removing the dipstick *before* running the engine, not after
- check tyre pressures once a week (look in your car's handbook for the correct pressures for your model)
- most cars now have sealed cooling systems, but check the level in the expansion bottle now and again. Remember to top it up with anti-freeze mixture, not just water
- most modern batteries don't need topping up, but find out if yours is an exception. If so, check it every 3 months and top up with distilled water if necessary
- check the water level in your windscreen washers regularly
- keep windscreen, all mirrors and lights clean (even if your car body isn't!)
- you must have anti-freeze in your car during the winter to prevent serious damage to your engine. It's easier to leave it in all year round, but it will need renewing every 3 years or so. Your garage can do this for you
- check your seatbelts regularly to ensure they aren't worn and that the belt mountings are firm
- if your car is over 3 years old, make sure it always has an up-to-date MOT certificate

....

TIP
Hose down underneath your car, particularly the wheel arches, before and after the winter months to prevent accumulated mud and salt causing rust

....

···

TIP
Some garages will carry out a pre-MOT check for you to
put right anything that would otherwise cause the car to
fail

···

Regular servicing

Your car handbook will tell you how frequently your car
needs servicing. Normally this is at certain mileage
intervals, but if your annual mileage is low the principle is
to base it on time periods between services. If you stick to
what the manufacturer recommends it will not only keep
your car in good running order, but it will minimise
breakdowns. Remember, though, that you yourself should
still carry out the basic checks I have listed above.

Garage tidiness

To keep your garage organised and to ensure you have as
much space as possible for your car:

- hang up everything you can
  - use pegboard
  - install shelves
- throw out anything old or unused for ages – all those nasty little tins of touch-up paint from two cars ago

....

TIP
If you have a lot of tools fixed to your garage pegboard, paint round them so you can see immediately which one is missing
....
TIP
If you do your own car maintenance or DIY, keep a first aid kit in the garage (for contents see p.136)
....

Bicycle lore

Nowadays many people are abandoning their petrol-consuming, laziness-encouraging cars and rediscovering the bicycle as a useful means of getting about locally. Your children probably have bicycles anyway, so it makes sense to know how to look after your wheels.

- keep tyres well pumped up
- check brakes regularly
- don't let your bike get rusty – keep it under cover and dry it off if it gets wet
- check once a week for any loose or wearing parts
- keep the lights in perfect order
- make sure the handlebars and saddle are at the best height for you
- always carry a basic tool kit which should include:
  - puncture repair kit
  - tyre valve
  - spare lamp bulbs
- padlock your bike when you leave it in the street

Car clutter and car essentials

Don't fill up your car with things you aren't likely to need and with rubbish that should be thrown out. If you do, you won't be able to find the things you really need, which are:

- car handbook
- maps
- local town guide
- AA or RAC handbook
- basic tools including a car jack and wheelbrace for changing wheels
- empty petrol can
- torch (check batteries regularly) or emergency light that can be run from the car battery
- squeegee for demisting outside of windows
- de-icer (winter only)
- duster, preferably anti-static, for inside of windscreen
- first-aid kit
- fire extinguisher (NB contents go off – keep yours recharged)
- tissues
- moist tissues (to clean hands after using petrol pumps)
- bin bag to collect any rubbish
- spare change for parking meters
- notepad and pen (essential in the event of an accident)

....

TIP

Always lock valuables and shopping in the boot. This only takes a second and deters thieves

....

Accident procedures

If you are unlucky enough to have an accident, follow this step-by-step procedure using the pen and pad which you should always keep handy in your car. As you may be in shock and therefore unable to think clearly after an accident, why not keep a copy of this checklist in your car?

- call an ambulance if anyone needs it
- take down the names and addresses of as many independent witnesses as you can – do this quickly or they will have left the scene
- call the police if anyone is injured, however slightly

- take the names and addresses of any other drivers involved in the accident, together with
  - their car registration numbers
  - the name and address of their insurers, plus the extent of their insurance cover and their policy number if possible (it's on their insurance certificate, which everyone should always have on them)
  - note the nature of the damage to the other person's car and any apparent injuries to driver and passengers
- make a rough sketch of the scene of the accident, noting relevant details such as:
  - was it dark or light?
  - approximate time of day
  - road conditions
  - in poor visibility, did all cars concerned have their lights on?
  - speed and position on the road, immediately before the accident, of all vehicles involved
- phone your insurance company

....
TIP
Don't fill your windscreen with stickers – if you can't see out of your own windows you'll end up having an accident
....

Quick checklist before taking your car out

- have you been drinking? Or are you over-tired? If so, don't drive – can someone else who is insured take the wheel?
- do you need petrol?
- do your tyres look up to pressure?
- are all your lights working?

- is your windscreen clean and can you see clearly in all your mirrors?
- have you got your AA/RAC membership card with you?

7 | Going Out on the Town – How to Make the Most of Your Social Life

This is meant to be the fun area of your life. If you do the right kind of organising and thinking ahead, you'll get a lot more pleasure out of it. Even entertaining at home, where you're doing all the work, can be enjoyable for you if you plan properly.

- do you ever invite guests who can't stand each other?
- do you ever provide delicious roast lamb scented with fresh herbs and garlic and forget there's a vegetarian coming?
- do you seem to spend all your time in the kitchen and emerge perspiring and cross to find you've missed all the gossip?

None of these need ever happen if you follow a few simple guidelines – you're probably already working them out for yourself if you've been absorbing the ideas on which this book is based.

PARTIES TO PLEASE EVERYONE

Entertaining at short notice

- does your husband bring colleagues back from the office without warning you?

- do your own two children turn into a gaggle of six or seven, all starving?

For emergency entertaining on these and similar occasions, make sure your kitchen contains
- all the basic ingredients (tomato concentrate, olive oil, onions, herbs, garlic, Parmesan cheese, pasta) for a delicious, if not gourmet, pasta dish
- at least two bottles each of red and white wine
- pretty paper napkins

Dinner parties that delight

....
TIP
Dinner parties are not the time for experiments. Always serve dishes you've cooked before
....

For dinner parties at home, keep a card index with the following information
- which guests were invited when, and with whom (that way you won't invite people too often or too infrequently, and they won't always be seeing the same faces)
- who doesn't get on with certain other people, so you don't invite enemies to the same party
- what food you served to whom (so they don't get the same meal, no matter how good, twice over)
- any food preferences/requirements (for e.g. vegetarians, non-Christians, dieters or friends who are just plain faddy!)

Plan your menus carefully, with an eye to your own enjoyment of the evening as well as that of your guests.
- a casserole such as coq au vin or boeuf bourguignon

that can happily wait in the oven for your guests (especially latecomers) is just as good as a roast that takes more of the cook's time and presence in the kitchen
- if you serve soup or pâté as a starter, accompany with a variety of interesting breads
- a green salad can be prepared in advance (just pour on the dressing at the last moment) and can't go cold or soggy like vegetables can
- one rich course in three is quite enough for most people
- puddings are fattening – to avoid embarrassing people who don't want to add inches but don't want to insult the cook either, stick to fresh fruit (as exotic as you can afford) and a range of prime cheeses
- if you have time to bake, serve the coffee with tiny home-made spicy biscuits rather than the ubiquitous chocolate mints – touches such as this make the meal seem special
- above all, BE PREPARED. Work out a timetable for the evening so virtually everything is cooked and ready before your guests arrive, leaving you time to bath and change and entertain them – after all, that's what it's all about!

CHILDREN'S PARTIES

Planning is essential here – bored children easily get fractious, and their parties shouldn't end up as free-for-alls!
- have at least one other adult to help out
- keep an eye out for the shy ones and try and encourage them to participate
- likewise don't let bullies/exhibitionists hog all the action

- make sure they all know where the loo is – put up some nice big signs and ensure the very young get any help they need
- kids love junk food but it's not very good for them – minimise the damage by providing low-fat vegetarian burgers and sausages and home-made tiny cheesy quiches
- watch out for any child with a queasy-looking face and help them out discreetly before there's an accident
- plan games meticulously in advance – always have something for them to do and never leave a breathing space (no matter how desperately *you* need one!)
- to ease the burden, consider hiring an entertainer such as a clown or conjurer for part of the time
- have lots of small prizes for games, wrap them interestingly, and try and make sure that every child wins something
- parties with a theme go down well – in the summer, try a teddy bears' picnic with teddy bear decorations, honey sandwiches and a teddy bear cake (and, of course, every child can bring their teddy)

CHRISTMAS WITHOUT THE HASSLE

Doing all that present-shopping in crowded stores is bad enough (though, if you're really organised, you'll have done it by the end of November), but having to do all the cooking and see that everyone's happy can really be too much for some people. Let's see what can be done to take the pain out of it.

- don't let anyone come into the kitchen (children, husbands, grandparents or pets) unless you say so – that way you won't get under each other's feet

- do as much of your food shopping as possible early, using your freezer wherever you can – you'll be avoiding steep prices and low stocks as well as the crowds
- do make sure the turkey is very well thawed before you cook it, and that it is then cooked all the way through – this is one of the prime causes of food poisoning and you don't want to spoil anyone's Christmas
- if you want a helper in the kitchen choose the most efficient member of your family – otherwise let children and grandparents entertain each other (gathering holly, putting up decorations, trimming the tree)
- not everyone wants Christmas pudding after the turkey – why not offer instead (or as well) a fresh fruit salad, perhaps with some exciting ingredients such as mangoes, lychees or cumquats? This is something that another member of your family could shop for and prepare
- don't let anybody eat or drink too much – but try and deal with it discreetly
- in case they do, make sure you've got a supply of Alka-Seltzer and aspirins
- if you haven't got a dishwasher, get the family to wash up after Christmas lunch. Turn a deaf ear to the sound of breakages – if you've prepared the meal, this is their turn and they must be left to get on with it
- then send everybody, people and dogs, out for a long walk. Go with them if you've got the energy (the fresh air will probably revive you), but if you're still too exhausted enjoy the peace and quiet and put your feet up with a book

···

TIP

Turkeys and Christmas puddings both need lengthy cooking. Work out a timetable in advance so that lunch is ready at the time you want it

···

TIPS

Buy and send Christmas cards early in December (any cards or presents for abroad may have to go earlier still if you want to use cheaper surface mail – check dates for various countries at the post office)

Keep a list of names and addresses of people to whom you send cards, and update it when they move, when they have an addition to the family or when someone dies – don't cause distress by addressing a card to a couple if one of them has died during the year

···

TIP

When sending out invitations, compile a list of names and tick off (yes/no) as you receive the replies

···

TIP

Always send a thank you note when people have entertained you, no matter how simply, and always send it the very next day

···

ON THE TOWN

An evening out – wonderful! Nothing to think about. I can just sit back and enjoy myself . . . Unfortunately it isn't quite true, if you think for a moment.

- do you forget the name of that new restaurant that had such a terrific write-up in the Sunday paper?
- can you remember the telephone number even of the old faithful trattoria you always seem to end up in?

- do you know the time of the last train – or do you spend ages trudging the streets for a taxi when they all seem to have gone into hibernation?
- do you ever leave your chequebook at home and then find when the bill comes that they don't take credit cards?

The list could go on and on, and most of us have been caught out on some or all of these things. With forethought, though, most of them can be avoided.

- clip out newspaper reviews of restaurants you want to try, and keep them in a file
- keep a card index of your regular restaurants' telephone numbers, together with a note of the days when they're closed
- keep details of last trains, late-night buses, taxi rank telephone numbers etc. in your handbag
- take all your forms of money out with you, or else find out in advance what is/is not acceptable
- if it's a special evening out, decide a few days ahead what you're going to wear and make sure it's clean and pressed
- book a hair appointment in advance if you want one
- arrange babysitters well in advance
- if you're going out straight from work, make sure you take with you that morning:
  - the right clothes and bag
  - the right shoes and tights
  - the right make-up
  - whatever jewellery you want to wear
  - heated rollers if you want to use them
  - deodorant/toothbrush/toothpaste (if not already in your desk drawers)

....

TIP
Keep the local theatre/cinema guide for that week/month
in your briefcase if you like to go out spontaneously
straight from work

....

8 | From Window Boxes to Green Acres – Care and Control of Your Garden

Your garden should never be a chore – it should enhance your family's life in some way, whether it's used mainly for your children to play in or you fill it with prize plants. The most important thing is to decide exactly what you want it to be. Do you need

- a play area for the kids and dogs
- extra space because the house is too small
- somewhere to grow vegetables to save on the housekeeping
- a place to eat outside and have barbecue parties
- a restful place to fill with plants?

Lucky you if you've got enough garden to accommodate all these requirements! The rest of us just have to get our priorities sorted out so that there are no clashes. If you've got children kicking a ball about all the time there's no point in trying to grow delicate plants, and if you want outdoor eating space you might have to give up some vegetable-growing space to build a decent-sized patio.

CHILDREN'S PLAY AREA

These are the kind of things you'll have to think about:

- sandpit (covered, so cats, dogs and foxes don't soil it)
- swing (made from an old tyre and set up over grass,

not concrete – these precautions will avoid cracked skulls if any child has an accident)
- space for ball games (as far away as possible from greenhouse/conservatory/house windows)
- paving for riding tricycles

HOUSE/DINING ROOM EXTENSION

You'll probably need to:
- build a patio large enough for a dining table and chairs
- buy garden furniture (teak keeps its looks in all seasons, though plastic and plastic-covered metal are cheaper and still rainproof)
- install a permanent barbecue if you enjoy this kind of food
- install outdoor lighting
- consider using up part of your garden for a conservatory/sun room

Some of these items are costly, but you'll probably be adding to the value of your home.

··

TIP
A pretty patio is an eye-catching feature, especially if you haven't had time to do the rest of the garden. Plant patio tubs cheaply with seeds for the summer: nasturtiums for colour, nicotines for scent in the evening
··

PLANTSMAN'S PARADISE

The traditional garden, with flowers and perhaps soft fruit and vegetables, can take a lot of looking after, or only a little. It depends on what you want in your garden, and on following certain sensible rules along the lines we've talked about in previous chapters.

....

TIP

Plant up pots or window boxes with herbs (parsley, thyme, rosemary, mint, chives) and keep them near the kitchen door for speedy snipping. But beware! Mint is very invasive, so always plant it in a pot on its own

....

Basic garden equipment

To look after the garden properly you'll need the following tools. Buy stainless steel if you can afford it – then there's no problem about rusting (though you should always dry off your tools and remove any soil and mud after use). Make sure secateurs fit your hand comfortably before you buy them, and that large items like digging forks and spades aren't too long or too heavy for you.

- secateurs (buy good ones that can be taken apart and sharpened – blunt blades damage plants and let in pests and diseases)
- hedging shears
- long-handled shears for lawn edging
- trowel
- small fork
- large fork for digging
- spade
- rake
- hoe
- lawn mower (mechanical/petrol/rotary)
- watering can

....

TIP

Get your lawn mower overhauled annually. Do it in the autumn and BE PREPARED – most people don't think about it until the following spring when the grass begins to grow again, so they have to join a queue

....

Also useful are:
- wheelbarrow
- lawn rake (with fan-shaped tines)
- electric hedge trimmers if you have a lot of hedges

TIP

Put a splash of bright paint (match pots are useful for this) on handles of garden tools. Then they won't get overlooked and left out in the rain to rust

TIP

Keep old egg boxes and plastic food containers for starting off seedlings – you don't have to buy special trays

Getting it all together

Just like when you're doing housework indoors, you don't want to be walking up and down the garden all the time looking for various bits and pieces. Buy a gardening apron with lots of pockets which will hold

- small tools such as secateurs

- garden twine
- garden ties
- seeds and bulbs

You also need

- a good tough pair of gardening gloves
- a kneeling pad

General hints for the would-be green-fingered

- oil and sharpen tools as shears often. It will make them last longer, and your garden tasks will be easier
- when storing tools in your garage or garden shed, hang up as much as possible and paint round the shapes so you can see instantly which tool is missing
- keep all poisonous substances tightly closed and out of reach of children and pets
- go through your bottles and packages of fertilisers, pest killers and so on regularly and dispose of unwanted stuff – but some of these are lethal and are therefore classed as toxic waste, so contact the council about how and where to get rid of them. Don't just flush them down the loo

....
TIP

Don't buy slug pellets if children or dogs use your garden. They look like sweets, but can be killers – to birds, too. Instead keep your grapefruit skins and put them cut side down around soft, vulnerable plants. First thing in the morning remove the slugs which will have collected underneath and either crush them or flush them down the loo
....
TIP

Give those thirsty plants the best chance! In summer, water in the evening when it's cooler, so less water will be lost through evaporation. And never water in full sun or the plants will get scorched. Window boxes, pots and tubs dry out more quickly than flower beds, so water them more frequently

....

Gardening calender

The right way to organise your garden activities is to set up a chart, which you can keep in your kitchen, garden shed or garage, with month-by-month activities marked on it. Select from the following calendar those items that interest or concern you, and enter them on your chart. This calendar is only an outline, and a good gardening book will fill you in on lots more details. Invest also in one or two good practical books (not necessarily the ones with the most colour pictures) containing specific information on the plants you want to grow (e.g. soft fruit, roses, clematis, greenhouse tomatoes). Remember that some activities go on over 2 or 3 months, and that conditions vary according to the part of the country you live in, because the seasons start earlier or later.

JANUARY
- check fences, arches, tall shrubs etc. – if weak and wobbly, heavy snow and wind could bring them down
- check that ties on trees are firm – if loosely planted with space at the roots they may end up waterlogged and die
- after a heavy snowfall, knock snow off shrubs and trees in case it breaks branches off
- put weedkiller on paths, taking care to keep it away from nearby plants

FEBRUARY

- get tools sharpened
- buy any insecticides, weedkillers and fertilisers that you need
- prune roses (do it later in the north)
- start hoeing out weed seedlings

MARCH

- start planting seeds for summer flowers and herbs – the packets tell you exactly when to plant and under what conditions
- plant gladioli and other bulbs for summer flowering
- start mowing the lawn if it's begun to grow

APRIL

- bring out garden furniture that's been in store over the winter
- start putting out grapefruit skins to catch slugs
- start buying trays of small summer annuals such as lobelia
- plant up hanging baskets and window boxes with geraniums, busy lizzies, lobelia etc.
- pay particular attention to getting rid of weeds, which are growing at their fastest now
- buy tomato plants and plant them up in grow-bags, staking or stringing them up once they are 6 inches high

MAY

- if the spring has been dry, water the garden regularly and continue doing so if the dry weather continues over the summer
- check plants (especially roses) for aphids and spray if necessary, continuing throughout the summer
- hoe regularly to deal with weeds, and continue throughout the summer

- thin and cut back any evergreen shrubs which need reshaping
- refill your swimming pool

JUNE
- dead-head roses regularly to encourage further flowers
- check climbers such as roses and clematis and tie in any new growth
- start feeding tomatoes, and water them up to twice a day in hot weather

JULY
- between now and the first frosts is the time to lay paths and patios – fresh concrete is damaged by frost
- continue weeding and watering

AUGUST
- heavy thunder showers may cause a crust on the soil which dries it out – break through it with a fork
- continue watering in dry spells and weeding
- check climbing plants again and tie in summer growth

SEPTEMBER
- plant all spring-flowering bulbs (daffodils, crocuses, snowdrops etc.) except tulips
- clean and put away all garden furniture that can rust or be otherwise damaged in frost and bad weather – deckchairs, plastic and metal furniture
- check plants for mildew and spray if necessary
- this month can be very windy – stake and tie up anything likely to be damaged

OCTOBER

- bring geraniums inside for over-wintering in a cool place before the first frosts get them
- put any terracotta pots under cover – if they get wet and then freeze in the frost they'll crack
- rake up dead leaves and dead plant material that harbour pests and burn them if you have space (or keep for Bonfire Night)
- remove any dead leaves etc. from gutterings to avoid leaks and flooding
- put a net over your fishpond to catch leaves – if they fall in they may kill the fish as they produce poisonous gases
- cut back whippy stems of roses (but don't prune completely until the spring)
- empty your swimming pool now or according to the installer's instructions
- after mowing the lawn for the last time clean and oil your mower and have it serviced (rotary mowers don't need servicing) before putting it away for the winter

NOVEMBER

- plant tulip bulbs after the first frost, which kills a disease in the soil to which they are prone
- if you want to grow vegetables, this is the month for digging – the frosts will help to break down the soil
- start planting new rose bushes, shrubs and young trees
- damp weather can make this a bad month for slugs – put out grapefruit skins again
- to prevent frost damage, cover the roots of camellias and rhododendrons with bin liners filled with straw and tied at the neck to prevent water getting in
- straighten lawn edges with a sharp spade
- remove any new fallen leaves

DECEMBER
- get your Christmas gifts or vouchers for gardening friends

....

TIP

Don't ruin lawns by walking on them in late autumn and winter, especially if you have heavy clay soil

....

TIP

Keep old tights to tie shrubs and young trees to stakes – they are less damaging than garden ties (and free!), and will quickly weather to blend in with the garden

....

TIP

If you have moved home and acquired a new garden, have a soil analysis done or buy a kit to do it yourself. This will tell you whether your soil is basically acid or alkaline, so you can buy plants that will do best in it

....

TIP

Remove weeds before they seed – if you wait until your garden is full of dandelion clocks it's too late: next year's crop is already assured!

....

TIP

Most plants (including roses) benefit from dead-heading – it stops them setting seed and they usually produce more flowers

....

TIP

Container-grown shrubs are more expensive than the bare-rooted kind, but you can plant them at any time of year

....

TIP

Never light a bonfire without first gently poking about in it with a broom handle – otherwise you may incinerate a hibernating hedgehog

....

TIP

Don't plant anything permanent in terracotta pots – the pots have to be taken indoors to avoid winter frost damage, and the plants may not survive the change in environment. Keep this kind of pot for summer annuals

9 | Expect the Unexpected – Emergency Routines

This is perhaps the ultimate example of my golden rule to BE PREPARED. Since emergency situations are often times of distress and worry, and you may not be thinking as straight as you usually do, there's all the more reason to have at your fingertips information on what to do and when.

GOING INTO HOSPITAL

This is something that most of us have to do at some stage in our lives. It needn't be an actual emergency as such, but if you're waiting your turn on an NHS list you may not have much time to organise things when the call does come. So try and do as much as possible in advance. As soon as you know a hospital stay is on the cards for you or a member of your family:
- get out the suitcase
- make a list of what will be needed

Here's a chart to make this task easier. It's designed to cover both sexes – just delete those items that aren't appropriate to you.

Things needed in hospital	Things to buy	Already packed
Dressing gown Bedjacket		

Slippers
Nightdress/
  pyjamas
Toilet bag
Toothbrush
Toothpaste
Soap
Sponge/flannel
Talc
Deodorant
Shampoo
Essential medicines
– such as
contraceptive pills
Hair dryer
Shaver/razor
Make-up bag
Brush and comb
Tissues
Towel
Spectacles
Books
Walkman and
  tapes
Address book
Family photos
Writing paper and
envelopes
Pen
Stamps

....

TIP
Give all medication you normally take to the nursing staff.
They will make sure that you get it, having checked that it
doesn't interfere with the treatment you're receiving

....

Add any other items which you know would make the person in question's stay in hospital more comfortable.

You will also need certain essential documents and other information:

- NHS medical card
- national insurance number if you are drawing benefit
- any pension, supplementary benefit or family income supplement order book
- private health scheme membership documents if you are going privately
- details of next of kin or person authorised to act for you

Remember also:

- make arrangements for your family to be looked after. This, depending on circumstances, can range from getting a friend or relative to stay, to making sure someone does the daily school runs and minds the kids until your husband/partner gets home from work
- if you're on social security, tell them the date when you're going to hospital. Look for leaflets on this at your local DSS office or library
- you are responsible for your personal laundry such as nightwear and other clothes – you may need to ask a friend to do you a favour and deal with this
- ask for a medical certificate if you need one for your employer or for insurance or national insurance purposes
- tell friends and relatives the wing and ward numbers/names so they can find you when they come to visit!
- tell them what the visiting hours are

Before leaving home

You'll need to go through the same procedures as when you go on holiday, but for convenience I'll list them here again:

- cancel the newspapers
- cancel the milk
- arrange with the post office or a neighbour to field your post
- unplug all electrical appliances except fridge/freezer (or turn them off at the mains if the fridge/freezer are on a separate circuit)
- make arrangements if necessary for someone to come in every day to turn on lights and water your plants
- arrange for pets to go to boarding kennels (if you can't get in at short notice, or you can't afford their fees because you're on a low income, a vet or animal welfare organisation will put you in touch with people who help out in such circumstances)

Children in hospital

When children have to stay in hospital, particularly if you can't be with them, it can be very upsetting for them. Here are a few do's and don'ts that may help if you and your child have to go through this potentially traumatic experience.

- try and stay in hospital with your child if possible
- if not, give the nurses a note containing any useful information about your child
- if the child is old enough, do tell him/her the truth (without any unnecessary details that might frighten) about what's going to happen and how long they will be away
- before they go, read them hospital stories or play hospital games so they can see it as an adventure

- give them lots of love so they don't feel they've been sent away as some sort of punishment
- pack their favourite toy or security blanket – it doesn't matter what it is if it makes them feel at home
- if you can't stay in hospital yourself, visit as frequently as possible

....

TIP
Teach your children their home phone number from a very early age, and show them how to dial 999 in the event of an emergency
....

....
TIP
Attach to your telephone a card containing the phone numbers of your doctor and a 24-hour plumber, also those of the gas and electricity emergency services
....
TIP
If you live alone (whatever age you are) and go away on holiday or a business trip, always make sure a friend or neighbour knows where you can be contacted in the event of house fire, burglary or other emergency. If you are new to an area and don't know anyone, tell the local police station
....
TIP
Whenever the family goes on holiday make sure a friend or neighbour has your holiday address and dates, your car registration number and approximate route if relevant, and (preferably) a key to the house
....
TIP
Foil those burglars! If you're regularly out of the house put hall and living room lights on a time switch so it looks as though someone's in
....

AVERTING PROBLEMS WITH THE ELDERLY

If you live alone and are elderly or disabled, or have a friend or relative in this category, ask the social services department of the local council if they run a
- community alarm scheme

This is a system which enables you to summon help in an emergency by means of a special link from your home to a centre which is manned day and night.

On p.35 I listed the kinds of foods which should always

be in an elderly person's kitchen cupboards in case they find themselves housebound for any reason. And it's a good idea to arrange to visit or phone an elderly person on a regular basis so you can check that all's well. But do fix this up tactfully – many elderly people quite understandably resent feeling they're being treated like children.

GAS LEAKS

If you smell gas in your home:
- don't light a match
- don't smoke
- don't switch on any lights
- open as many windows as possible
- call the gas board

....

TIP

Fit a smoke alarm in your sitting room, and check (and preferably empty) all ashtrays before you go to bed. Never smoke in bed – you may fall asleep with a lighted cigarette in your hand

....

FIRE

Fires in the home

- don't be afraid of dialling 999, no matter how small the fire. There are inflammable and lethal substances in every home, and most fire deaths are caused by inhaling noxious fumes and gases

- throwing a blanket over a fire to stifle it is often more effective than water
- get all people and pets outside as fast as possible
- with electrical fires, never use a liquid-based fire extinguisher – if in doubt, don't. Don't touch the appliance's own switch or plug, but turn off the mains switch as quickly as you can
- burning fat/oil is the major cause of domestic fires
  - don't fill your chip pan more than one-third full of oil
  - don't let it over-heat
  - if it does catch fire, don't put water on it. Instead, quickly soak a towel/tea towel in water, wring it out, and throw it over the pan to cover it completely (this starves the flames of oxygen). Turn off the ring or electric plate and don't touch the pan for at least an hour.

What to do if your car catches fire

- get out of the car if you are in it!
- if the fire is under the bonnet use your fire extinguisher (which is not, of course, a water-based one)
- if the fire gains hold, retreat to a safe distance and rely on your insurance – your car is more replaceable than you are

NB What to do if you have an accident in your car is dealt with on p.103.

BURGLARS

If you are unlucky enough to come home and find you've had unwelcome visitors:

- if the burglars are still there, don't be tempted to 'have a go' – panic can turn any burglar violent
- phone the police
- don't touch anything in case you destroy fingerprints
- when the police arrive, try and work out what's missing and give them a list
- report the loss to your insurance company
- have all locks changed as quickly as possible (your insurance company may insist on it anyway)

....

TIP
Put your name and address on valuables such as videos with a special marker pen whose writing is only visible in ultra-violet light – most stationers sell them
....
TIP
Fit window locks on all windows – they're not entirely foolproof but they do discourage burglars who want to be in and out quickly
....
TIP
Keep a list of all your valuables, with accurate detailed descriptions and photographs wherever possible. This may speed up the settlement of your insurance claim and help the police to recover your property
....
TIP
Make sure the cover on your house contents policy is high enough – remember that while most things depreciate in value, antiques and jewellery go up
....
TIP
Make sure you know where the electricity main switch and all stopcocks are in your home
....

WATER WHERE IT SHOULDN'T BE

Burst pipes

Try and avert this unwelcome and messy situation by lagging and insulating thoroughly. Most modern central heating programmers enable you to leave the heating on low if you are away during cold weather, and many have a fail-safe device which automatically turns the heating on if the temperature falls to a dangerously low level. If you don't have central heating you have more of a problem – a friendly neighbour may be able to help out here if you let him or her have a key. If you do get caught out and your pipes burst:

- turn off the water at the main stopcock
- if the burst is in a cold water pipe leading from a tank, bale out the tank to minimise the flood damage and turn off the stopcock near the tank (if you haven't got one, consider having one fitted)
- call a plumber as quickly as possible
- if water has leaked into or near electrical sockets, turn off the electricity at the mains and call an electrician

Washing machine leaks

This seems to happen to everyone at one time or another. If you're the victim

- turn off the water supply to the machine
- if the rubber hose has gone, disconnect and replace it
- if not, call in a repair man
- if water has leaked into or near electrical sockets, turn off the electricity at the mains and call an electrician

- remember to claim on your insurance for items such as damaged furniture legs and kitchen units and ruined rubber underlay

FIRST AID

We dealt with a very basic first aid kit in Chapter 2, mainly aimed at coping quickly with kitchen burns, scalds and cuts. A more complete kit would include the following:

- liquid antiseptic
- calamine lotion
- cotton wool
- plasters

- sterile dressings
- sterile eye dressings
- tubular bandage
- crepe bandage
- painkillers such as Paracetamol
- cream for insect bites
- tweezers for removing splinters
- fine needle (sterilise in antiseptic before use) for the same purpose
- blunt-ended scissors for cutting dressings
- safety pins

Kitchen, bathroom and car are all candidates for having a first aid kit. Have one in your garage, too, if any member of your family does their own car maintenance or is a DIY fanatic.

....
TIP
Keep in your handbag/wallet a note with name, address and phone numbers (daytime and evening) of your next of kin, in case of accident
....

The best way to find out about first aid is to go on a course (contact your local St John's Ambulance office). Here are one or two do's and don'ts – mostly the latter, because well-meaning but unskilled first aid can often cause more harm than good.
- if you suspect head/neck/back injuries, don't move the patient as paralysis might result – never remove an injured motorcyclist's crash helmet for this reason
- don't move people with suspected broken bones
- don't give alcohol to people who may be in shock – a cup of hot sweet tea is best
- keep accident victims warm to ward off the effects of shock

- don't attempt to stop bleeding with a tourniquet unless you have had proper instruction – you can easily block the circulation, which can be dangerous. If it's a limb that's affected, try and hold it upwards so the pumping action of the arteries is reduced and less blood is lost

TEST YOUR ORGANISATIONAL SKILLS

Tick how many of the following routines you now follow since reading this book. Five marks for every yes.

	Yes	No
Do you freeze your milk or orange juice?		
Do you put the things you need for the next day ready in the hall?		
Are your letters to post waiting in the hall?		
Do you have back-ups of the following: • kitchen rolls • toilet rolls • toothpaste • soap • light bulbs? (score 1 point for each)		
Is your shopping list up-to-date?		
Do you know your whole family's social life for the next week?		
Have you weeded any clothes from your wardrobe?		
Do you have at least two blank greetings cards in your home?		

Top score 40
30–40. Well done, you really want to be organised.
20–30. You're trying, but need to recap.
Less than 20. Read this book again!